JN422063

Guide to the Culinary Industry

Kang, Kyung Jae

BAEKSAN
Publishing Co.

Preface & Acknowledgements

This book is the tenth one which I have developed since I served as a professor. When this book was first considered, my objective was to have a publication that would offer various contents, data and information related to the culinary industry which are needed to broaden our students' views on the industry. Actually I have perceived the word "culinary industry" is now being used in other countries outside Korea from two to three years ago. Since then I have thought of producing a book connected with the culinary industry. In the consideration of the trend of culinary industry in Korea, we're at the right time to use the word "culinary industry." So I have researched and collected data and articles connected with the culinary industry for the last 4 months. Based on these materials, I developed 'Guide to the Culinary Industry.'

This book has a total of 15 chapters which are Introduction to the Culinary Industry, Career Guide and Essential Culinary Terms, Positive Attitude the toward Culinary Industry, New Phenomena and New Concepts, Using Herbs and Spices, The World's Healthiest Foods, Dedicated to Lifelong Learning, Introduction to Korean Cuisine, Introduction to Chinese Cuisine, Introduction to Japanese Cuisine, Introduction to Western Cuisine, Introduction to Food Service Management, Introduction to Food Styling, Introduction to Wine and Introduction to Coffee. In Chapter 1 Introduction to the Culinary Industry, there are four sections which are Definition of Culinary Industry, Exploring Industries related to the culinary industry, Analysis of Scopes among the Hospitality, Culinary, Food Service, Restaurant and Catering Industry, and Culinary Industry Overview. Chapter 2 Career Guide and Essential Culinary Terms consist of four sections which deal with Job Prospects, Building a Career in the Culinary Industry, All about Chefs and Essential Culinary Terms. Chapter 3 Positive Attitude toward the

Culinary Industry has three sections which cover The Professional Chef, Uniform, and Lab Requirements and Uniform & Personal hygiene Code. Chapter 4 New Phenomena and New Concepts include seven sections which are Slow food, Molecular Gastronomy, Food Miles, Sustainable Cuisine, Food Deserts, Culinary Tourism and Culinology®. In Chapter 5 Using Herbs and Spices, there are four sections and you will explore What are Spices and Herbs?, Do Herbs and Spices add Any Nutritive Value to Foods?, Using Herbs and Spices and Storing Herbs and Spices. Chapter 6 The World's Healthiest Foods have five sections which provide Olive Oil (Spain), Soy (Japan), Yogurt (Greece), Lentils (India) and Kimchi (Korea). In Chapter 7 Dedicated to Lifelong Learning, there are three sections which cover Culinary Education, Taking an Overseas Internship and English Interview Tips. In Chapter 8 Introduction to Korean Cuisine, there are three sections which introduce Korean Food, Korean Cooking in America, and Korean Dish 'may cure bird flu'. Chapter 9 Introduction to Chinese Cuisine has two sections which provide Yin-Yang Foods and Chinese Food: History, Popularity, Healthy. In Chapter 10 Introduction to Japanese Cuisine there are two sections, and you will learn The Characteristics of Japanese Cuisine and Japanese Restaurant Recommendation Program (Draft). Chapter 11 Introduction to Western Cuisine has two sections which focus on The Great Chefs and Special Expressions related to Western Cuisine. In Chapter 12 Introduction to Food Service Management, there are three sections which prepare you for Menu Trends in 2010, A Partial List to Control Expenses and The Dangers of Eating Fast Food. Chapter 13 Introduction to Food Styling is splitted into three sections which cover Things that Food Stylists do, Tricks that Food Stylists perform, and Job Education & Training that Food Stylists receive. Chapter 14 Introduction to Wine has six sections and you will explore Wine Production and Consumption, What does Sommelier do?, Wine Facts and Information, Wine Tasting Guide, Wine and Food Paring, and Role of Wine in Preparing a Dish. In Chapter 15 Introduction to Coffee, there are four sections which examine Coffee Production and Consumption in the World, Knowledge about Coffee, Coffee Trivia and An interesting Story of Coffee. At the end of every chapter references are added.

I did major nothing relating to English Literature. This book is the tenth book among the books written by me and published before. I'm sure this book will act as an inspiration to always learn more, and encourage to gain confidence in studying English my student chefs who are eager to be successful in the culinary industry.

Ten years ago I was deeply impressed and shocked by the New Professional Chef 6th(ed.) which was given as a gift by one of my students, Mr. Yang, Kyu Mo. In the book there is a didactic sentence that can't be forgotten even in my dream that is "A true chef is, among other things, a lifelong student, a teacher, a craftsman, a leader, and a manager." The book has influenced tremendously and will influence me continuously. As the development of food and cuisine has never been completely one-sided, so culinary education is not one-sided. Therefore student chefs have to influence the persons engaging in culinary education, and vice versa. I want to strongly emphasize that an interaction between student chefs and the persons engaging in culinary education is of great importance in culinary education.

In writing this book I have already promised to myself more improved and updated book will be published in the next edition listing a body of information pertaining to the culinary industry.

I want to thank and acknowledge the following individuals for their help and assistance in the development of this book. The persons I have recognized here are some of those nice individuals from the culinary industry who were willing to share their experiences, knowledge, and expertise.

My special thanks to: Professor Kim, Jong Young, Hyejeon College; Professor Cho'i Song San, Hyejeon College; Professor Kim, Yong Mun, Hyejeon College; Professor Yi, Chae Ch'ol, Hyejeon College; Professor Yeo, Kyung Ok, Hyejeon College; Professor Park, Chan Kuk, Hyejeon College; Cho, Nam Kon, Director of Chonpok MyungGa; Lee, Kye Kyung, Director of NamPoMyeonOk; Mun, Sung Kwon, Owner/Chef SamjungBonjum; Yeo, Kyung Rae, President of Hongbo Chinese Restaurant; Yu, Dae Jun, President of KBTC(Korea Barista Training Center); Chong, Kyong Sung, Owner/Chef of Chonsu-sa Restaurant; Kim, Chun Hwi, Consultant of Seosan small business development center;

Oh, Su Kun, Consultant of Seoul support center for Veterans; Kwak, Jae Hun, Proprietor of OUTBACKSTEAKHOUSE; Lee, Jae Kun, President of Lee Jae Kun Coffee School; Cho'i, Byung Uk, Team Manager of Elimsung Chinese Restaurant; Lee, Chong Hak, Team Manager of Chabudai; Seo, Sang Yun, Team Manager of F&B Division, Daemyung Leisure Industry Co., ltd.; Bang, Hyo Sang, Team manager of Business Team, M Castle; Se Dae Hui, Director, Hosko.

I am grateful for the important materials provided by Cho, Byung Sook, ex-my student of Department of Hotel Culinary Arts, Hyejeon College who is President of Hongsung Cooking & Bakery School.

I offer my thanks and gratitude to the below individuals for their help and assistance in the development of this edition.

My special thanks to: President Yi, Chae Ho, Hyejeon College; Ex-Vice President Yang, Chae Gil, FoodCulture of SAMSUNG EVERLAND INC.; Dr. Yun, Sung Ro, Yun's Surgical Clinic; Dr. Kim, Man Gil, Gil's Dermatological Clinic; General Manager Yu, Je Ch'un, Sheraton WalkerHill Hotel; President Kang, Min Soo, Korea Food and Tourism Association: Pedro Y.K. Yu, General Manager of Sales&Marketing, Lee Kum Kee Trading Ltd.; Fergus J. Han, Assitant Manager of Business Development, Lee Kum Kee Trading Ltd.; Chong, So In, Lee Kum Kee Trading Ltd.; Teacher Kim, Hang Sup, my close friend; Professor Shin, Sang Chun, Howon University; Professor Oh, Nam Sun, Kongju University; Professor In, Man Jin, Chongwoon University; Professor Yu, Kyong, Min, Soonnch'on University; Professor Han, Min Su, Hyejeon College; Professor Yi, Yong Hwan, Hyejeon College; Professor Kim, Kyung Im, Hyejeon College; Proefessor Park, Sang Hye; Professor Chong, Won Hee, Masan College; Professor Lee, Nam Mi; Professor Mun, Ok Sun; Preseident Im, Kum Ran, Hwangje Food Academy; Preseident Yi, Young Ju, Seoch'on Cooking Academy; Vice-Preseident Chong, Hye Jung, Hongsung Cooking & Bakery School; Kim, Kyung Tae, Co-President of Hongju Funeral Service; Yi, Jun Seok, President of Kidjob Education Center; Professor Yi, Sang In; Kim, Young Su, Manager of Learning Center, Kookmin Bank; Hwang, Sun Man, ex-teaching assistant of Department of Hotel Culinary Arts and FoodCulture of

SAMSUNG EVERLAND INC.; Park, Ki Ho, ex-teaching assistant of Department of Hotel Culinary Arts, Hyejeon College; Dr. Oh, Ch'ol Hwan, Kongju University; Yeo, Woon Hyuk, Bakery of Grand Hyatt Seoul; Ka, Hui Chin, Cho, Hye Chin, An Young Hye, Cho, Han pyo, teaching assistant of Hyejeon College; Yi, Bok Ku; Shin, Hyun Ok; Yi, Du Won; Ahn, Duk Kyun; Chon, Byong Wan; Cha'e Hui Duk; Yi, Ki Sun; Chang, Won Kyung; Chang, Kyung Un; Chang, Hong Kyung; Ji, Sung Jin; Cho'l, Tae Uk; Ku, Bon Uk; Yun, Chun Ho; Im, Yong Hwan; Chong, Ji Sun; Kim, Sang Jin; Heo, In Bum; Chu, Sung Un; Ham, Hye In; Kim, Nam Dong; Yi, Young Chun; Yi, Chong Won; Im U Sun; Kim, Ja Kun; Sung, Hyun Pil; Kim, Sang U; Park, Chang Sun; Cho'l, Yun Ho; Kwak, Chong Min; Yi, Chan Ho; Shin, Ji Su; Kim, Ki Yup, Hyejeon College.

I would like to thank my family, my wife Ko, Yon Suk, my first son, Kang, Byung Su(Bill), my only daughter, Kang, Dong Ok(Diana), and my second son, Kang, Duk(David) for their hard work, dedication, sacrifice, and assistance. Bill is attending College of Oriental Medicine, Kyungwon University. Diana is attending College of Dentistry, Wonkwang University. Also I always thank for Bill, Diana, and David, a high school student, who are being grown up well and working very hard. Especially I want to appreciate my wife, Ko, Yon Suk, who has worked hard for our family, helping me with the manuscript and with a precious and invaluable dedication to accomplish a better publication. As a result I complete the development of this book.

God bless you!

Kang, Kyung Jae

Supervisor, Major in Japanese Cuisine, Division of Hotel Culinary Arts & Foodservice, Hyejeon College

Contents

If you want one year of prosperity, plant corn.

If you want ten years of prosperity, plant trees.

If you want one hundred years of prosperity, educate people.

Chinese proverb

Chapter 01

Introduction to the Culinary Industry

World map indicating the Human Development Index
(based on 2007 data, published on October 5, 2009)

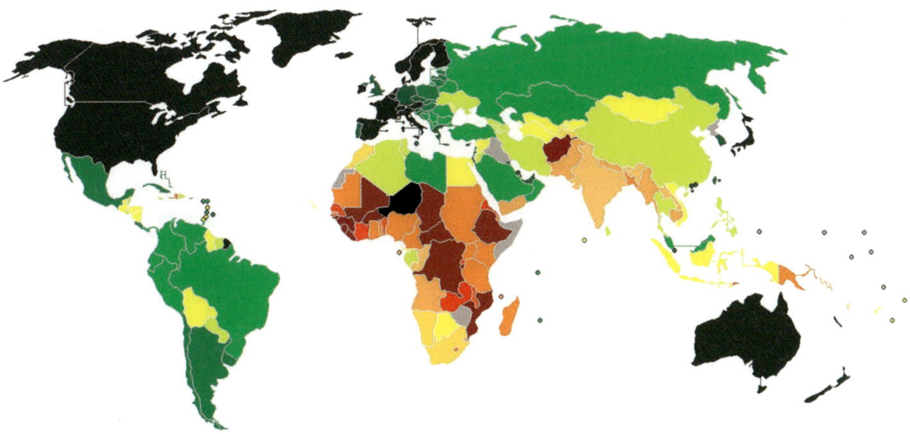

Legend

0.950 and over	0.700–0.749	0.450–0.499
0.900–0.949	0.650–0.699	0.400–0.449
0.850–0.899	0.600–0.649	0.350–0.399
0.800–0.849	0.550–0.599	under 0.350
0.750–0.799	0.500–0.549	Data unavailable

The Human Development Index (HDI) is an index used to rank countries by level of "human development", which usually also implies whether a country is developed, developing, or underdeveloped.
(Source : http://en.wikipedia.org/wiki/Human_Development_Index)

The illiterate of the 21st century will not be those who cannot read and write, but those who cannot learn, unlearn and relearn.

Alvin Toffler (1928-)

1. Definition of Culinary Industry

The culinary field is a vast, diverse industry. When we are discussing about culinary industry, our first task is to know the meanings of culinary, arts, and culinary arts. To look up definitions of the term "culinary" is based upon six dictionaries on the internet. Table 1-1 shows us that the term "culinary" means something connected with cooking (which means the activity of preparing food and food itself), cookery (which means the art or practice of preparing food and kitchen), kitchen and food, that is to say the culinary has four meanings such as the activity of preparing food, the art or practice of preparing food, kitchen and food itself, (Education.yahoo, Encarta.msn, Merriam-webster, Dictionary.cambridge, En.wiktionary, Whatscookingamerica, n.d.).

A dictionary definition of the term "art" is skill that is attained by study, practice, or observation (Education.yahoo, n.d.), but generally it is defined as the ability or skill involved in doing or making something (Answers, n.d.). Therefore, the term "culinary arts" is defined as all about the art of cooking, as all about being concerned with the way food is prepared and served, and as all about making things easier and all functions more efficient in the kitchens.

On the other hand, the term "industry" is generally used to describe any grouping of businesses that share a common method of generating profits, such as the "movie industry", the "automobile industry", or the "cattle industry" It is also used specifically to refer to an area of economic production focused on manufacturing which involves large amounts of upfront capital investment before any profit can be realized, also called "heavy industry" (Info.abaara, n.d.).

Hence the term "culinary industry" is defined as organized economic activities connected with the production and provision of food and beverages that are not prepared in the home, and other related economic activities based on food and beverages and kitchens. In foreign countries the word "culinary industry" seen on the home pages of many culinary schools, colleges and universities, in many articles of journals related to culinary industry, and so on, is too numerous to be counted (Culinaryprograms, n.d.; Jwu, 2008; Acfchefs, n.d.; Zahari, et al., 2009; Johnson, 2009). But in Korea the word "culinary industry" is seen only on 4 places. Here are examples.

1) In introducing a major in culinary industry management, within School of Hotel & Tourism Management, Sejeong Cyber University, the word “culinary industry” is used in the name of the major (Sejeong Cyber University, n.d.).

2) In introducing a department of foodservice & culinary industry, within Division of Culture & Industry, Wonkwang Health Science University, the word “culinary industry” is used in the name of the department (Wonkwang Health Science University, n.d.).

3) In introducing "Bachelor of Food Cuisine," or “식품조리학과” in Korean, Hoseo Technical College, the word “culinary industry” is mentioned (Hoseo Technical College, n.d.).

4) In introducing four qualifications about Industrial Engineer Cook (Korean food), or 조리산업기사 (한식) in Korean, Industrial Engineer Cook (Chinese food) or 조리산업기사 (중식) in Korean, Industrial Engineer Cook (Western food) or 조리산업기사 (양식) in Korean, Industrial Engineer Cook (Japanese food) or 조리산업기사 (일식) in Korean, and Industrial Engineer Cook (Blowfish) or 조리산업기사

(복어조리) in Korean, the word "culinary industry" is mentioned (Human Resources Development Service of Korea, n.d.).

▌Table 1-1▐ Meanings of Culinary

<table>
<tr><th rowspan="2">Meaning / Source</th><th colspan="2">Cooking</th><th colspan="2">Cookery</th><th rowspan="2">Kitchen</th><th rowspan="2">Food</th></tr>
<tr><th>Activity</th><th>Food</th><th>Art</th><th>Kitchen</th></tr>
<tr><td rowspan="2">① American Heritage Dictionary of the English Language</td><td rowspan="2"></td><td rowspan="2"></td><td>The art or practice of preparing food</td><td>A place for cooking</td><td rowspan="2">Of or relating to a kitchen</td><td rowspan="2"></td></tr>
<tr><td colspan="2">Of or relating to cookery</td></tr>
<tr><td rowspan="2">② Encarta® World English Dictionary, North American Edition</td><td>The process or activity of preparing food for eating</td><td>Food that has been prepared for eating
Ex.)
She doesn't like my cooking.</td><td rowspan="2"></td><td rowspan="2"></td><td rowspan="2"></td><td rowspan="2">relating to food</td></tr>
<tr><td colspan="2">relating to cooking</td></tr>
<tr><td rowspan="2">③ Merriam-Webster's Online Dictionary, 11th Edition</td><td rowspan="2"></td><td rowspan="2"></td><td>The art or practice of cooking</td><td>An establishment for cooking</td><td rowspan="2">of or relating to the kitchen</td><td rowspan="2"></td></tr>
<tr><td colspan="2">of or relating to cookery</td></tr>
<tr><td rowspan="2">④ Cambridge International Dictionary of English</td><td>Preparing or cooking food</td><td>Ex.)
I love my dad's cooking (=the food that he cooks).</td><td rowspan="2"></td><td rowspan="2"></td><td rowspan="2">connected with kitchens</td><td rowspan="2"></td></tr>
<tr><td colspan="2">connected with cooking</td></tr>
<tr><td>⑤ Wiktionary</td><td colspan="2">Relating to the activity of cooking</td><td colspan="2">Relating to the practice of cookery</td><td>Of, or relating to a kitchen</td><td></td></tr>
<tr><td>㉖ Linda's Culinary Dictionary</td><td colspan="2">anything to do with cooking</td><td colspan="2"></td><td></td><td></td></tr>
<tr><td colspan="7">Remark : When the word "culinary" is entered in "the Word or phrase Box" and clicked the "Search" button in OneLook Dictionary Search (http://www.onelook.com/), the first 5 dictionaries the author references are seen and the last one is connected with culinary field.
(Source : http://education.yahoo.com/, http://encarta.msn.com/, http://www.merriam-webster.com/, http://dictionary.cambridge.org/, http://en.wiktionary.org/, http://whatscookingamerica.net/)</td></tr>
</table>

2. Exploring Industries related to the Culinary Industry

Various definitions on restaurant industry, catering industry, hospitality industry and food service industry are explored. These definitions explored form the basis for the comparison among scopes of each industry. Let's explore these industries in more detail.

1) Food Service Industry

As stated in an article on Wikipedia, the foodservice (or food service) industry (US English; catering industry in British English) encompasses those places, institutions, and companies responsible for any meal eaten away from home. This industry includes restaurants, school and hospital cafeterias, catering operations, and many other formats. This industry is called "food service industry" in American English-speaking countries, but it is called as "catering industry" in British English-speaking countries. The former is chosen by the author for consistency and unity of terms used in this text.

According to a research by IFDA (International Foodservice Distributors Association). foodservice is the industry that serves any food that is not prepared in the home (IFDA, n.d.).

As stated in a report by Companiesandmarkets, foodservice is defined as the sale of food and drinks for immediate consumption either on the premises from which they were bought, or in designated eating areas shared with other foodservice operators, or in the case of takeaways transactions, freshly prepared food for immediate consumption (Companiesandmarkets, n.d.).

North American Industry Classification System (NAICS) gives a number, 722, to this Food Service Industry (Food Services and Drinking Places). Industries in the Food Services and Drinking Places subsector prepare meals, snacks, and beverages to customer order for immediate on-premises and off-premises consumption. There is a wide range of establishments in these industries. Some provide food and drink only; while others provide various combinations of seating space, waiter/waitress services and incidental amenities, such as limited entertainment. The industries in the subsector are grouped based on the type and level of services provided. The industry groups are full-service restaurants; limited-service eating places; special food services, such as food service contractors, caterers, and mobile food services; and drinking places.

Food and beverage services at hotels and motels; amusement parks, theaters, casinos, country clubs, and similar recreational facilities; and civic and social organizations are included in this subsector only if these services are provided by a separate establishment primarily engaged in providing food and beverage services.

Excluded from this subsector are establishments operating dinner cruises. These establishments are classified in Subsector 487, Scenic and Sightseeing Transportation because those establishments utilize transportation equipment to provide scenic recreational entertainment (Census, 2007).

Meanwhile, 722 Food Services and Drinking Places subsector defined by North American Industry Classification System (NAICS) includes the various industries

(Census, 2007) in which young student chefs can be employed after a College or University. Let's find out what's what.

① 7221 Full-Service Restaurants

This industry group comprises establishments primarily engaged in providing food services to patrons who order and are served while seated (i.e., waiter/waitress service) and pay after eating. Establishments that provide these type of food services to patrons with any combination of other services, such as carryout services are classified in this industry.

② 72211 Full-Service Restaurants

This industry comprises establishments primarily engaged in providing food services to patrons who order and are served while seated (i.e. waiter/waitress service) and pay after eating. These establishments may provide this type of food services to patrons in combination with selling alcoholic beverages, providing takeout services, or presenting live non theatrical entertainment.

③ 7222 Limited-Service Eating Places

This industry group comprises establishments primarily engaged in providing food services where patrons generally order or select items and pay before eating. Most establishments do not have waiter/waitress service, but some provide limited service, such as cooking to order (i.e., per special request), bringing food to seated customers, or providing off-site delivery.

④ 72221 Limited-Service Eating Places

This industry comprises establishments primarily engaged in (1) providing food services where patrons generally order or select items and pay before eating or (2) selling a specialty snack or nonalcoholic beverage for consumption on or near the premises. Food and drink may be consumed on the premises, taken out, or delivered to customers' location. Some establishments in this industry may provide these food services (except snack and nonalcoholic beverage bars) in combination with selling alcoholic beverages.

⑤ 722211 Limited-Service Restaurants

This U.S. industry comprises establishments primarily engaged in providing food services (except snack and nonalcoholic beverage bars) where patrons generally order or select items and pay before eating. Food and drink may be consumed on premises, taken out, or delivered to customers' location. Some establishments in this industry may provide these food services in combination with selling alcoholic beverages.

⑥ 722212 Cafeterias

This U.S. industry comprises establishments, known as cafeterias, primarily engaged in preparing and serving meals for immediate consumption using cafeteria-style serving equipment, such as steam tables, a refrigerated area, and self-service nonalcoholic beverage dispensing equipment. Patrons select from food and drink items on display in a continuous cafeteria line.

⑦ 722213 Snack and Nonalcoholic Beverage Bars

This U.S. industry comprises establishments primarily engaged in (1) preparing and/or serving a specialty snack, such as ice cream, frozen yogurt, cookies, or popcorn or (2)serving nonalcoholic beverages, such as coffee, juices, or sodas for consumption on or near the premises. These establishments may carry and sell a combination of snack, nonalcoholic beverage, and other related products (e.g., coffee beans, mugs, coffee makers) but generally promote and sell a unique snack or nonalcoholic beverage.

⑧ 7222131 Ice Cream and Soft Serve Shops

Establishments primarily engaged in selling ice cream and/or frozen custard for immediate consumption.

⑨ 7222132 Frozen Yogurt Shops

Establishments primarily engaged in selling frozen yogurt for immediate consumption.

⑩ 7222133 Donut Shops

Establishments primarily engaged in selling donuts, for consumption on or off the premises.

⑪ 72221331 Donut Shops, Baking on Premises

Establishments primarily engaged in selling donuts baked on the premises.

⑫ 72221332 Donut Shops, No Baking on Premises

Establishments primarily engaged in selling donuts not baked on the premises.

⑬ 7222134 Bagel Shops

Establishments primarily engaged in selling bagels, including bagel sandwiches, for consumption on or off the premises. Establishments primarily engaged in selling bulk bagels to retail customers are also included.

⑭ 7222135 Coffee Shops

Establishments primarily engaged in selling freshly brewed coffee, for consumption on or off the premises. Establishments providing beverage teas are also included.

The sale of food frequently accounts for a substantial portion of the sales of these establishments.

⑮ 7222136 Cookie Shops

Establishments primarily engaged in selling cookies.

⑯ 7222137 Other Snack and Nonalcoholic Beverage Bars

Establishments primarily engaged in selling specialty snacks and beverages such as pretzels, sodas, and juices from permanent sites for immediate consumption on or near the premises.

⑰ 7223 Special Food Services

This industry group comprises establishments primarily engaged in providing one of the following food services:

(1) at the customers' location; (2) a location designated by the customer; or (3) from motorized vehicles or nonmotorized carts.

⑱ 72231 Food Service Contractors

This industry comprises establishments primarily engaged in providing food services at institutional, governmental, commercial, or industrial locations of others based on contractual arrangements with these type of organizations for a specified period of time. The establishments of this industry provide food services for the convenience of the contracting organization or the contracting organization's customers. The contractual arrangement of these establishments with contracting organizations may vary from type of facility operated (e.g., cafeteria, restaurant, fast food eating place), revenue sharing, cost structure, to providing personnel. Management staff is always provided by the food services contractor.

⑲ 72232 Caterers

This industry comprises establishments primarily engaged in providing single event-based food services. These establishments generally have equipment and vehicles to transport meals and snacks to events and/or prepare food at an off-premise site. Banquet halls with catering staff are included in this industry. Examples of events catered by establishments in this industry are graduation parties, wedding receptions, business or retirement luncheons, and trade shows.

⑳ 72233 Mobile Food Services

This industry comprises establishments primarily engaged in preparing and serving meals and snacks for immediate consumption from motorized vehicles or non motorized carts. The establishment is the central location from which the caterer route is serviced, not each vehicle, or cart. Included in this industry are establishments primarily engaged in providing food services from vehicles, such as hot dog cart, and ice cream truck.

㉑ 7224 Drinking Places (Alcoholic Beverages)

This industry group comprises establishments primarily engaged in preparing and serving alcoholic beverages for immediate consumption.

㉒ 72241 Drinking Places (Alcoholic Beverages)

This industry comprises establishments known as bars, taverns, nightclubs or drinking places primarily engaged in preparing and serving alcoholic beverages for immediate consumption. These establishments may also provide limited food services.

2) Restaurant Industry

According to definition by PSIC (Philippine Standard Industrial Classification), the restaurant sub-sector, on the other hand, includes places that serve food and drinks, be it self-service or full-service. This covers a range of services including fine dining speciality restaurants, fast food outlets, canteens, and food courts (Edralin & Castillo, 2001).

NRA defines restaurant industry as all meals/snacks prepared away from home, including all takeout meals and beverages (Riehle, 2008).

3) Catering Industry

As stated in the travel industry dictionary, catering is defined as the act of providing food and drink for an event, and as the department responsible for providing such services (Hometravelagency, n.d.). As stated in an article on Wikipedia, catering is the business of providing food service at a remote site.

On the other hand, North American Industry Classification System (NAICS) codes this catering industry with a number, 72232. This industry comprises establishments primarily engaged in providing single event-based food services. These establishments generally have equipment and vehicles to transport meals and snacks to events and/or prepare food at an off-premise site. Banquet halls with catering staff are included in this industry. Examples of events catered by establishments in this industry are graduation parties, wedding receptions, business or retirement luncheons, and trade shows (Census, 2007).

4) Hospitality Industry

As stated by DeShields, the hospitality industry is defined as the activity of providing lodging, food and beverage, and recreational services, which include but are not limited to hotels, motels, clubs, casinos, restaurants, recreation facilities, tourism, cruise lines, and theme parks (DeShields, n.d.).

As stated in a research by PPRC (The Pacific Northwest Pollution Prevention Resource Center), the hospitality industry covers a wide ranging number of services and activities. It includes travel related services such as lodging, restaurants, food services and convention centers. Also included are entertainment services including golf courses, sports arenas, amusement parks, movie theaters, playhouses, concert venues, tour services, and national and state parks, to name but a few (PPRC, 1998).

In a report on the economic impact of San Antonio's hospitality industry, Butler and Stefl used the lines of business defined by the North American Industrial Classification System to define the scope of hospitality industry in of San Antonio. Table 1-2 shows that hospitality industry is separated into 4 subsectors such as lodging subsector, restaurants and catering subsector, transportation and travel subsector, and entertainment subsector based on the North American Industrial Classification System (Butler and Stefl, 2008).

Figure 1-1 shows that among lodging subsector, restaurants and catering subsector, transportation and travel subsector, and entertainment subsector of hospitality industry, the restaurants and catering subsector made the largest contribution to the local economy, accounting for 42.2% of the total economic impact, or $4.6 billion. The vast majority of this large impact was due to full-service or limited-service restaurants and eating places ($1.9 billion and $2.2 billion respectively), with the remainder coming from catering services and drinking establishments (Butler and Stefl, 2008).

We can see restaurants and catering subsector plays a key role in the overall economic impact on a city or country. So the culinary industry is an exciting and dynamic field, offering a number of opportunities for those who have a passion for cooking and strong creative skills. Let's get into the world of culinary industry.

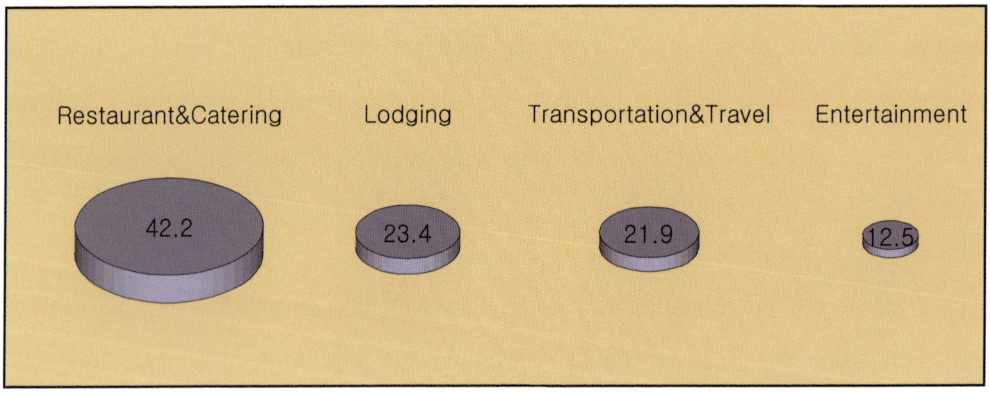

Figure 1-1 The Economic impact of the Hospitality Industry in 2008
(Source : http://www.sariverfoundation.org/downloads/visitor_study.pdf)

Table 1-2 NAICS Codes For The Hospitality Industry

Lodging	7211 Hotels, motels, etc. 7212 RV parks and recreational camps
Restaurants and Catering	7221 Full service restaurants 7222 Limited-service eating places 7223 Special food services 7224 Drinking places

Transportation and Travel	48111 Scheduled air transportation 48521 Interurban and rural bus transportation 48551 Charter buses 48599 Other ground passenger transportation 48711 Scenic and sightseeing transportation 48811 Airport operations 53211 Passenger car rental and leasing 56152 Tour operators 56159 Other travel arrangement services 81293 Parking lots and garages
Entertainment	51213 Motion picture exhibition 7111 Performing arts companies 71121 Spectator sports 7113 Promoters of performing arts 7115 Independent artists, writers and performers 7121 Museums, historical sites, zoos, etc. 71311 Amusement and theme parks 71312 Amusement arcades 71391 Golf courses and country clubs 71399 Other amusement and recreation

(Source : http://www.sariverfoundation.org/downloads/visitor_study.pdf)

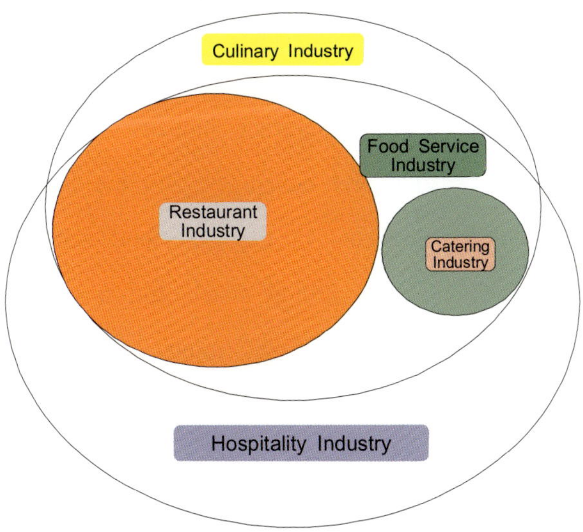

Figure 1-2 Comparing scopes among the hospitality industry, culinary industry, food service industry, restaurant industry, and catering industry

3. Analysis of Scopes among the Hospitality, Culinary, Food Service, Restaurant and Catering Industry

As stated by Armstrong and others, the food service and culinary industry come under the umbrella of the hospitality services (Armstrong, Callie, et al., 2006). Thus it's no doubt that the culinary industry, food service industry, restaurant industry, and catering industry belong to the hospitality industry.

Based upon the definitions on the food service industry, restaurant industry, catering industry, and hospitality industry explored, the food service industry can be literally defined as an industry that provides food and beverages outside the home. The restaurant industry can be defined an industry related to a place where food and beverages are sold and served to customers. The catering industry is an industry related to the business of providing food and drink for an event at a remote site. The restaurant industry doesn't include the catering industry. The restaurant industry is one thing, and the catering industry is another.

The food service industry and restaurant industry are similar in that both industries prepare and serve food and beverages. But the food service industry is different from the restaurant industry in that the food service industry includes establishments primarily engaged in selling snack and nonalcoholic beverage and other related products (e.g., coffee beans, mugs, coffee makers), which the restaurant industry excludes, and in that the food service industry comprises establishments primarily engaged in providing one of the following food services: (1) at the customers' location (food service contractors); (2) a location designated by the customer (caterers); or (3) from motorized vehicles or nonmotorized carts (mobile food services), which the restaurant industry excludes. Thus the restaurant industry comes under the umbrella of the food service industry.

On the other hand, Section 1 in Chapter 1 shows the term "culinary industry" is defined as organized economic activities connected with the production and provision of food and beverages that are not prepared in the home, and other related organized economic activities based on food, beverages and kitchens.

In that both the culinary industry and the food service industry prepare and serve food and beverages, both industries are similar. But the culinary industry is different from the food service industry in that the culinary industry includes other related economic activities based on food, beverages and kitchens, which the food service industry excludes. In terms of related economic activities based on food, beverages and kitchens. people in the culinary industry enter into wider areas than those in the food service industry. In addition, there are more career opportunities in the culinary industry than in the food service industry because people in the culinary industry possess culinary skills as stated in Section 2 in Chapter 2.

Table 1-3, as stated in Section 2 in Chapter 2, shows that people with a degree in culinary arts can have career opportunities involving cooking or not involving cooking.

In Table 1-3, among opportunities primarily engaged in cooking, foodstylists don't belong to the food service industry. Among opportunities hardly engaged in cooking, food writers (cookbook authors, food critics), media personalities, salespeople (sales representatives), educators, research & development directors (research and development chefs, menu development chefs, recipe/food tester), and culinologists don't belong to the food service industry, either.

Table 1-3 Career opportunities

Opportunities primarily engaged in cooking	① Chef Owners (Chef/Owners, Chef & Owners, Chef-Owners) ② Executive Chefs ③ Baking & Pastry Chefs (Dessert Specialist, Bread and Pastry Baker, Pastry Chef or Patissier) ④ Food Preparation and Serving Supervisors ⑤ Institutional Chefs ⑥ Personal Chefs (Private Household Cooks, Private Chefs, Freelance Chefs) ⑦ Catering Chefs (Caterers and Event Planners, Catering Specialists) ⑧ Food Stylists
Opportunities hardly engaged in cooking	① Restaurateurs (Restaurant Owners) ② Food Writers (Cookbook Authors, Food Critics) ③ Entrepreneurs ④ Media Personalities ⑤ Food Service Managers (Restaurant Managers) ⑥ Food and Beverage Managers (Wines & Spirits Specialists, Food and Beverage, Supervisors) ⑦ Food and Beverage Controllers (Purchasing Agents) ⑧ Consultants (Kitchen Designers, Food Consultants, Restaurant Designers, Design specialists) ⑨ Salespeople (Sales Representatives) ⑩ Educators ⑪ Research & Development Directors (Research and Development Chefs, Menu Development Chefs, Recipe/Food Tester) ⑫ Culinologists

Among opportunities hardly engaged in cooking, entrepreneurs, consultants (kitchen designers, food consultants, restaurant designers, design specialists), salespeople (sales representatives), educators, research & development directors (research and development chefs, menu development chefs, recipe/food tester), and culinologists have nothing to with the hospitality industry, and don't belong to the hospitality industry, either. The hospitality industry the comprises culinary industry with the exception of those job opportunities.

To conclude, the restaurant industry doesn't include the catering industry. The restaurant industry is one thing, and the catering industry is another. The catering industry comes under the umbrella of the food service industry, the restaurant industry under the umbrella of the food service industry, and again the food service industry under the umbrella of the culinary industry. The culinary industry, food service industry, restaurant industry, and catering industry come under the umbrella of the hospitality industry, which includes the culinary industry with the exception of those job opportunities. Figure 1-2 shows comparing scopes among the hospitality industry, culinary industry, food service industry, restaurant industry, and catering industry.

Note

- upfront : frank and honest
- capital : money and possessions, especially a large amount of money used for producing more wealth or for starting a new business
- journal : a serious magazine or newspaper which is published regularly, usually about a specialist subject
- premises : the land and buildings owned by someone, especially by a company or organization
- designated : selected or named for a duty
- takeaway (US takeout) : a meal cooked and bought at a shop or restaurant but taken somewhere else, often home, to be eaten, or the shop or restaurant itself
- transaction : an instance of doing business of some kind, e.g., a purchase made in a shop or a withdrawal of funds from a bank account

- NAIC : The Office of Management and Budget's North American Industry Classification System (NAICS) is a system for classifying establishments (individual business locations) by type of economic activity in Canada, Mexico, and the United States. Its purposes are: (1) to facilitate the collection, tabulation, presentation, and analysis of data relating to establishments, and (2) to promote uniformity and comparability in the presentation and analysis of statistical data describing the North American economy. NAICS is used by Federal statistical agencies that collect or publish data by industry. It is also widely used by State and local agencies, trade associations, private businesses, and other organizations.
- incidental : less important than the thing something is connected with or part of
- amenity : something, such as a swimming pool or shopping centre, that is intended to make life more pleasant or comfortable for the people in a town, hotel or other place
- contractor : a person or company that arranges to supply materials or workers for building or for moving goods
- amusement park (theme park) : a large permanent area for public entertainment, with entertaining activities and big machines to ride on or play games on, restaurants, etc., all connected with a single subject
- civic : of a town or city or the people who live in
- services : facilities for travelers available at intervals along a highway, e.g. stores, restaurants, toilets, and a service station
- patron : a person who uses a particular shop, restaurant, hotel, etc., especially regularly; a customer
- to order : according to the requirements of a specific customer
- dispense : to give out things, especially products, services or amounts of money, to people
- display : a collection of objects or pictures arranged for people to look at, or a performance or show for people to watch
- bagel : a small, hard roll of bread in the shape of a ring
- pretzel : a hard salty biscuit that has been baked especially in stick or knot shapes

- permanent : describes something that exists or happens all the time
- revenue : the income that a government or company receives regularly
- canteen : a place in a factory, office, etc. where food and meals are sold, often at a lower than usual price
- vehicle : a machine usually with wheels and an engine, which is used for transporting people or goods on land, especially on roads
- luncheon : formal for lunch
- trade show (trade fair) : a large event at which companies show and sell their products and try to increase their business
- lodging : a temporary place to stay
- arena : a large flat area surrounded by seats used for sports or entertainment
- playhouse : a theatre. This is now only used in the names of theatres.
- venue : the place where a public event or meeting happens
- to name but a few : 몇 가지만 말하자면
- account for sth : to form the total of something

4. Culinary Industry Overview

1) Booming industry

Research by the Bureau of Labor Statistics suggests that the culinary industry will experience one of the largest increases in new jobs until 2016. Jobs for chefs, cooks, and food preparation workers may increase by 11% through 2016, in other words, figures predict there will be about 351,000 new jobs over that span; however, competition should be keen for jobs in the top kitchens of higher end restaurants. Although job growth will create many new positions, the overwhelming majority of job openings will stem from the need to replace workers who leave this large occupational group. Many chef, cook, and food preparation worker jobs are attractive to people seeking first-time or short-term employment, additional income, or a flexible work schedule. Employers typically hire a large number of part-time workers, but many of these workers soon transfer to other occupations or stop working, creating numerous openings for those entering the field. At higher end restaurants, the fast pace, long hours, and high energy levels required to succeed also cause some top chefs and cooks to leave for other jobs, creating job openings (Ctculinary, n.d.; Livecareer, 2009).

It's no surprise, then, that the culinary industry employs an estimated 12.8 million people (more than 9 percent of those employed in the U.S.), making it the nation's largest employer outside of government. And, in the next decade alone, the U.S. culinary industry is predicted to add 2 million new positions, creating the need for well-trained professionals, for total culinary career employment of 14.8 million by 2017 (Tellefsen, n.d.; Jwu, 2008).

2) Lucrative industry

As stated in Section 2 in Chapter 1, the food service industry comes under the umbrella of the culinary industry, and agin the restaurant industry comes under the umbrella of the food service industry. Since there is no culinary industry statistics. restaurant industry statistics is used instead (NRA, 2009). Four out of five consumers agree that going out to a restaurant is a better way to use their leisure time than cooking and cleaning up. The dollar signs prove it (Tellefsen, n.d.). Let's look at the following analysis (See Table 1-4; 1-5; Figure 1-3; 1-4; 1-5).

Table 1-4 2009 Restaurant Industry Overview

Sales	$566 Billion
Locations	945,000
Employees	13 million
Restaurant-Industry Share of the Food Dollar	48%

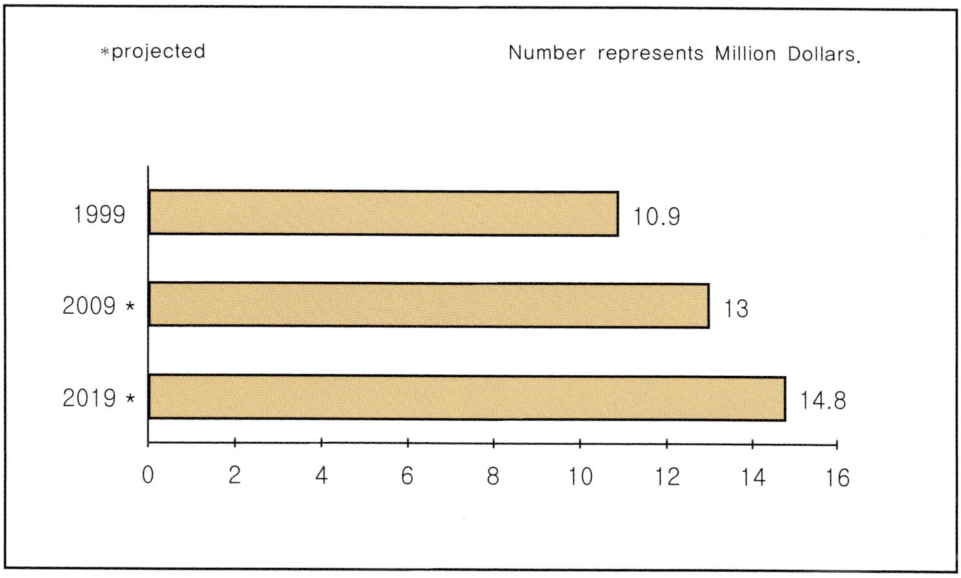

Figure 1-3 Total Restaurant Industry Employment

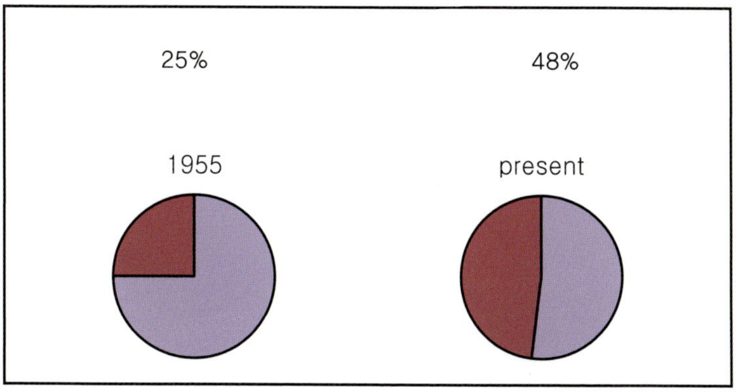

Figure 1-4 Restaurant Industry Share of the Food Dollar

Table 1–5 Industry Sales Projection, 2009: $566 Billion

Type of Establishment	2009 Estimated Sales (Billions)
Commercial	$516.0
Eating places	$377.9
Drinking places	$17.1
Managed services	$40.1
Lodging-place restaurants	$27.9
Retail, vending, recreation, mobile	$52.9
Other	$49.9

① Restaurants : An essential part of daily life

Restaurants will provide more than 70 billion meal and snack occasions in 2009.

On a typical day in America in 2009, more than 130million individuals will be foodservice patrons.

68% of adults said their favorite restaurant foods provide flavor and taste sensations which cannot easily be duplicated in their home kitchen.

② Restaurants : Cornerstone of career opportunities

The restaurant industry employs an estimated 13 million people, or 9% of the U.S. workforce (See Table 1-3; Figure 1-3).

The restaurant industry is expected to add 1.8 million jobs over the next decade, with employment reaching 14.8 million by 2019 (See Table 1-3; Figure 1-3).

Nearly half of all adults have worked in the restaurant industry at some point during their lives, and more than one out of four adults got their first job experience in a restaurant.

Eating-and-drinking places are extremely labor intensive-sales per full-time-equivalent employee were $73,436 in 2007, which is much lower than most other industries.

One-quarter of eating-and-drinking-place firms are owned by women, 15% by Asians, 8% by Hispanics and 4% by African-Americans.

Eating-and-drinking places employ more minority managers than any other industry.

Fifty-seven percent of first-line supervisors/managers of food preparation and service workers in 2007 were women, 16% were of Hispanic origin and 14% were African-American.

③ Restaurants : Small Businesses with a large impact on our nation's economy

Restaurant-industry sales are forecast to advance 2.5% in 2009 and equal 4% of the U.S. gross domestic product.

The overall economic impact of the restaurant industry is expected to exceed $1.5 trillion in 2009.

Every dollar spent by consumers in restaurants generates an additional $2.02 spent in our nation's economy.

Each additional dollar spent in restaurants generates an additional $0.82 in household earnings throughout the economy.

Every additional million dollars in restaurant sales generates an additional 33 jobs for the economy.

Eating-and-drinking places are mostly small businesses—with 91% having fewer than 50 employees.

More than seven out of 10 eating-and-drinking place establishments are single-unit operations.

Average unit sales in 2006 were $867,000 at fullservice restaurants and $715,000 at limited-service restaurants.

④ Restaurants by the Numbers

$1.5 Billion : Restaurant-industry sales on a typical day in 2009

69% : Percent of adults who said purchasing meals from restaurants, take-out and delivery places makes it easier for families with children to manage their day-to-day lives.

52% : Percent of adults who said they are likely to make a restaurant choice based on how much a restaurant supports charitable activities and the local community.

27% : Percent of adults who said that when it comes to choosing a restaurant, they are paying more attention to coupons and value specials than they were two years ago.

60% : Percent of quickservice customers who said they would patronize quickservice restaurants more frequently if the restaurant offered discounts for dining at off-peak times of the day.

27% : Percent of adults who said they have used the Internet to search for nutrition information about restaurant food.

70% : Percent of adults who said they are more likely to visit a restaurant that offers locally produced food items.

75% : Percent of fullservice customers who said they would patronize fullservice restaurants more frequently if they offered discounts for dining on less busy days of the week.

51% : Percent of fullservice customers who said they would be likely to utilize an option of delivery directly to their home or office if offered by a fullservice restaurant.

60% : Percent of adults who said they are more likely to visit a restaurant that offers food that was grown or raised in an organic or environmentally-friendly way.

76% : Percent of adults who said they are trying to eat healthier now at restaurants than they did two years ago.

88% : Percent of fullservice customers who said there are more healthy options available at sit-down tableservice restaurants than there were two years ago.

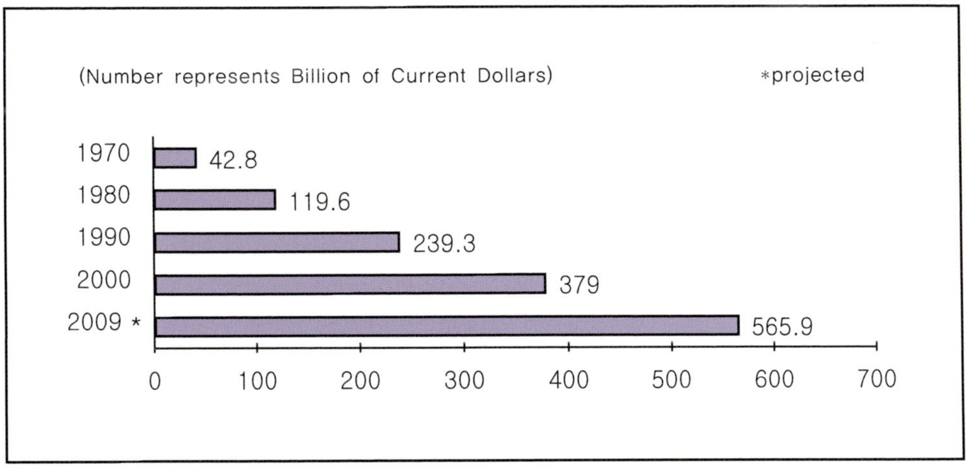

Figure 1-5 Restaurant Sales since 1970 (Food & Drink Sales)

Note

- span : the period of time that sometimes exists or happens
- keen : extreme or very strong
- stem from sth : to start or develop as the result of something
- transfer : to change to a different job, team, place of work, etc., or to make someone do this
- lucrative : (especially of a business, job or activity) producing a lot of money
- occasion : A need created by a particular circumstance
- sensation : a physical feeling caused by having one or more of the sense organs stimulated
- duplicate : to make an exact copy of something
- cornerstone : something of great importance which everything else depends on
- labor intensive : Industries and methods which are labour-intensive need a lot of workers
- hispanics : connected with Spain or Spanish-speaking countries, especially those countries in Latin America
- minority : any small group in society that is different from the rest because of their race, religion or political beliefs, or a person who belongs to such a group
- gross domestic product : the total value of all goods and services produced within a country in a year, minus net income from investments in other countries
- trillion : the number 1 000 000 000 000
- charitable : giving money, food or help free to those who are in need because they are ill, poor or have no home
- special : (mainly US) a product that is being sold at a reduced price for a short period

References

통계청, 2008, 한국표준산업분류(KSIC : Korean Standard Industrial Classification), Retrieved Jan. 16, 2010 from http://kostat.go.kr/kssc/

Armstrong, Callie, et al., 2006, Culinary Concepts, First Edition 2006, Student Guide, The Multistate Academic and Vocational Curriculum Consortium, Inc. Retrieved Dec. 27, 2009 from http://www.okcimc.com/hospitality/CCUnit01.pdf

Butler, Richard V. and Mary E. Stefl, 2008, "The ECONOMIC IMPACT of San Antonio's HOSPITALITY INDUSTRY," San Antonio Area Tourism Council, Retrieved Jan. 16, 2010 from http://www.sariverfoundation.org/downloads /visitor_study.pdf/benchmark/2009/html/naicsdef.html

Census, 2007, "Monthly Retail Trade and Food Services NAICS Codes, Titles, and Descriptions. Retrieved Dec. 26, 2009 from http://www.census.gov/mrts/www

Companiesandmarkets, "Cost Foodservice-BRIC (Brazil, Russia, India, China) Industry Guide, Retrieved Dec. 27, 2009 from http://www.companiesandmarkets.com /print-friendly-cost-foodservice-bric-(brazil,-russia,-india,-china)-industry-guide-163687.aspx

Ctculinary, "Fast Track to Culinary Career Success,"Retrieved Jan. 14, 2010 from http://www.ctculinary.com/careerpaths/index.htm

Culinaryprograms, "A History of Le Cordon Bleu," Retrieved Dec. 27, 2009 from http://www.culinaryprograms.com/cordon.htm

Culinaryed, "What Should I Consider Before Attending Culinary School?," Retrieved Jan. 9, 2010 from http://www.culinaryed.com/

DeShields, Gregory L., "Choosing a Career in the Hospitality Industry," Retrieved Dec. 26, 2009 from http://hotel-industry.learnhub.com/lesson /13362-choosing-a-career-in-the-hospitality-industry

Edralin, Divina M. and Paulynne Castillo, 2001, "An In-depth Study on the Hotel and Restaurant Industry In the Philippines," August 17, Retrieved Dec. 27, 2009 from http://dirp3.pids.gov.ph/ris/taps/tapspp0105.pdf

Human Resources Development Service of Korea, "국가자격종목별상세정보," Retrieved Jan. 29, 2010 from http://www.q-net.or.kr/

IFDA, "Foodservice Distribution: Connecting the Foodservice Industry," Retrieved Dec. 27, 2009 from http://www.ifdaonline.org/webarticles/anmviewer.asp?a=622&z=38

Info.abaara, "Industry," Retrieved Jan. 5, 2010 from http://info.abaara.com/pac/Industry

Johnson, Erik, 2009, "Deciding to Start a New Career in the Culinary Arts," Dec. 18, Retrieved Jan. 9, 2010 from http://www.goarticles.com/cgi-bin/showa.cgi?C=2392818

Livecareer, 2009, "Careers in the Culinary Industry Draw Spotlight," Sep. 11, Retrieved Jan. 14, 2010 from http://www.livecareer.com/news/Travel-Entertainment-Culinary /Careers-in-the-Culinary-Industry-Draw-Spotlight_$$01002.aspx,

Miseenplace, "Catering Management Jobs," Retrieved Feb. 2, 2010 from http://www.miseenplace.co.uk/catering-management-jobs.html

NRA, 2009, "Restaurant Industry Pocket Factbook," Retrieved Jan. 14, 2010 from http://www.restaurant.org/pdfs/research/2009Factbook.pdf

PPRC, 1998, "Pollution Prevention in the Hospitality Sector," August, Retrieved Dec. 26, 2009 from http://www.pprc.org/pubs/hosptlty.cfm

Riehle, Hudson, 2008, "Restaurant Industry 2008 and Beyond," Rhode Island Hospitality & Tourism Association Economic Outlook Breakfast, Oct. 21, Retrieved Jan. 5, 2010 from www.rihospitality.org/pdf/Hudson Riehle.ppt,

Tellefsen, Robyn, "A Sampling of the Culinary Industry," Retrieved Jan. 14, 2010 from http://www.degrees-in-culinary.com/article /a-sampling-of-the-culinary-industry/890/

Zahari, Mohd Salehuddin Mohd, et al., 2009, "Gastronomy: An Opportunity for Malaysian Culinary Educators," International Education Studies, May, 2(2), Retrieved Dec. 26, 2009 from http://ccsenet.org/journal/index.php/ies/article/view/1687/1632

Retrieved Feb. 3, 2010 from http://www.hometravelagency.com/dictionary/

Retrieved Jan. 13, 2010 from http://encarta.msn.com/encnet/features/dictionary/

Retrieved Jan. 14, 2010 from http://en.wikipedia.org/wiki/

Retrieved Jan. 14, 2010 from http://www.answers.com/topic/craft

Retrieved Jan. 14, 2010 from http://education.yahoo.com/,

Retrieved Jan. 14, 2010 from http://www.merriam-webster.com/,

Retrieved Jan. 14, 2010 from http://en.wiktionary.org/,

Retrieved Jan. 14, 2010 from http://whatscookingamerica.net/

Retrieved Jan. 14, 2010 from www.acfchefs.org

Retrieved Jan. 29, 2010 from http://outfood.wu.ac.kr/

Retrieved Jan. 29, 2010 from http://uni.shoseo.ac.kr/department/food1.asp.

Retrieved Jan. 9, 2010 from http://www.merriam-webster.com/dictionary/indispensable

Retrieved Jan. 29, 2010 from http://portal.sjcu.ac.kr/jsp/subject/new_subject.jsp?p_showmenu=3&s_showmenu=3&p_ifrmurl=/jsp/subject/guide/new_hotel_guide06.jsp

Chapter 02

Career Guide and Essential Culinary Terms

Getting into the world of the culinary industry is not as easy as everybody thought it is, but life in the culinary industry is incredibly exciting, rewarding and taxing.

1. Job Prospects

Before getting into the world of the culinary industry, three aspects must be considered. Those aspects are opportunities, weaknesses, and traits/talents. The first 2 aspects are inevitable characteristics that the culinary industry has, and the other aspect is one that young students must develop and have while in a college or an university.

1) Opportunities

Coming straight out of cooking school, most starting chefs are able easily to find work in the culinary field, allowing them to hone their skills as they continue to build fine careers in the culinary industry. People will always need food for their survival, and as long as there are appetites, people will seek better and more interesting foods to appease their palate. You can be the chef that fulfills those needs (Culinaryed, n.d.).

A restaurant, however, is by no means the only option for a work environment. There are plentiful opportunities for chefs outside of the restaurant setting. You could work in hospitality, on a cruise or at a resort; as an industry chef in the kitchens of schools, businesses, hospitals, cafeterias, and other institutions; as a personal chef in someone's home; you could specialize as a pastry chef or baker; the possibilities are endless. For these reasons it is difficult to pin down the general job description of someone working in the culinary field. However, that can be good news because it means that unique opportunities abound (Careereducationadvisor, n.d.).

Most people eat three times a day, and when they are not actively eating, they are considering what and where their next meal will be. Most industries do not experience this sort of stability when it comes to the demand for their products. The culinary industry is one of the fastest growing industries in the world. The culinary industry itself can be just as diverse as the professionals it's comprised of. The culinary industry is unique because, as long as you create a dish that appeals to at least a small segment of the population, you are bound to be successful. In fact, the culinary industry can be the excellent place to start and make your living (Careereducationadvisor, n.d.; Smith, 2009).

While television shows and magazines have helped popularize this field in recent years, many of these would-be chefs come into the business as a second career. People who have a passion for food and cooking are good candidates for working in the culinary industry. If you are one of those who love spending time in preparing different foods or like to work with people in food decoration then making a career in culinary industry can surely be the most appropriate decision (Smith, 2009, Articlesbase, 2009). From positions in restaurants, resorts, spas and cruise lines to careers in nutrition, food product development or as a celebrity chef —opportunities in the expansive culinary industry are limited only by your imagination (Jwu, 2008).

2) Weaknesses

Many restaurant and institutional kitchens have modern equipment, convenient work areas, and air conditioning, but kitchens in older and smaller eating places are often not as well designed. Kitchen staffs invariably work in small quarters against hot stoves and ovens. They are under constant pressure to prepare meals quickly, while ensuring quality is maintained and safety and sanitation guidelines are observed (Newfuturesdc, 2009).

The culinary industry does not adhere to a 9 to 5 schedule, five days a week. Work hours in the culinary industry may include early mornings, late evenings, holidays, and weekends. In particular the weekend evening hours are the boom time in the culinary industry. In order to become a successful master chef, you must be available and at your best during the culinary industry's peak hours. Serving a fine meal for dinner is one of the main goals, and this often makes life difficult for those with families or loved ones. Many executive chefs regularly work 12-hour days because they oversee the delivery of foodstuffs early in the day, plan the menu, and prepare those menu items that take the most skill (Newfuturesdc, 2009). In order to become a successful chef, you must be able to work around such obstacles and resign yourself to living outside of the weekend (Culinaryed, n.d.). But

3) Traits/Talents

You must be highly organized in order to schedule food preparation, coordinate the work of the kitchen staff, and ensure that quality food supplies are available in the right quantities. In addition, you should be people-oriented and a team player, as you will be working closely with kitchen and service staff. Chefs are often caught in stressful situations, but you must remain courteous, tactful, patient and calm.

As the presentation of a meal is almost as important as the preparation of its ingredients, you should have a creative and artistic flair. A keen sense of taste and smell are also necessary, as is good hand-eye coordination. Since you will be handling food for a large portion of the day, you need to exhibit high standards of personal hygiene and cleanliness (Skillsalberta, 2009).

Note

- aspect : one part of a situation, problem, subject, etc
- trait : a particular characteristic that can produce a particular type of behaviour
- appease : To satisfy or relieve
- palate : a person's ability to taste and judge good food and wine
- pin sth down : to discover exact details about something
- abound : to exist in large numbers
- bound : [after verb] certain or extremely likely to happen
- would-be : wanting or trying to be
- celebrity : someone who is famous, especially in the entertainment business
- quarter : an area of a town where a particular group of people live or work or where a particular activity happens
- adhere to sth : to continue to obey a rule or have a belief
- obstacle : something that blocks you so that movement, going forward or action are prevented or made more difficult
- resign yourself to sth : to make yourself accept something that you do not like because you cannot change it
- courteous : polite and respectful; well-mannered
- tactful : careful not to say or do anything that could upset someone
- flair : natural ability to do something well
- hand-eye coordination : the ability to do things that involve your hands and eyes working together, for example catching a ball, passing something through a needle, or drawing pictures

- coordination : the act of making all the people involved in a plan or activity work together in an organized way
- hygiene : the degree to which people keep themselves or their environment clean, especially to prevent disease

2. Building a Career in the Culinary Industry

The culinary industry has and will continue to have excellent job opportunities. Millions of meals are prepared daily in restaurants, hotels, schools, and health care facilities. Upon graduation from professional culinary programs at a culinary college or university, you will be able to pursue a number of rewarding careers. The possibilities are endless. Many of the following career opportunities are available for students completing an associate degree in culinary arts. Just think what you could do with an associate's degree or a bachelor's degree! Let's start a new career in the culinary industry (See Table 1-3)!

1) Career opportunities involving cooking.

① Chef Owners (Chef/Owners, Chef-Owners, Chef & Owners) : Becoming a chef is one of the most rewarding professions, so much more when owning and running your own restaurant. Some chefs who have worked for successful restaurants are made to own their own restaurant and some are not. However, becoming a chef and owning a restaurant requires not only a huge investment, but also a creative mind, a passionate heart and a motivated work ethic. For those of you who are thinking of opening and running your own restaurant, it is necessary to remember that owning and operating a restaurant receive acclaim as a chef-owner and entails considerable risks.

Perhaps some day young students, who are experienced, highly motivated persons and learn knowledge about costs, marketing, and the more which are requisite for a restaurant's success, will have its own Michelin-starred chef-owned restaurant.

② Executive Chefs : They are in charge of all kitchen staff and the meals that are prepared. They oversee all kitchen operations and handle duties such as ordering supplies, keeping accounts, and planning menus. They are also responsible for food preparation and styling, recipe development, and meal creation. Executive chefs ensure appealing presentation as well as good taste. In large restaurants with numerous staff, executive chefs may do little of the actual cooking. But they work long hours nevertheless (Cookingschools, n.d.).

③ Baking & Pastry Chefs (Dessert Specialist, Bread and Pastry Baker, Pastry Chef or Patissier) : The pastry chef prepares pastries and desserts, as well as bread and other baked goods. In larger restaurants, pastry chefs may supervise a pastry team in a separate kitchen. Pastry chefs are often in charge of the dessert menu, and will research, create, and test new recipes. They may also oversee other dessert-related items, such as dessert wines, dessert beverages, and gourmet cheese platters (Edu.chefsblade, n.d.).

④ Food Preparation and Serving Supervisors : They oversee the kitchen and non-kitchen staff in a restaurant or food service facility. They may also oversee food preparation workers in fast food, cafeteria, or casual dining restaurants, where the menu is fairly standard from day to day, or in more formal restaurants, where a chef provides specific guidelines and exacting standards on how to prepare each item (Careers.collegetoolkit, n.d.).

⑤ Institutional Chefs : They are employed in schools and cafeterias usually work with a limited menu but with large quantities (Skillsalberta, 2009).

meals your way
personal chef service

⑥ Personal Chefs (Private Household Cooks, Private Chefs, Freelance Chefs) : Personal chefs and private household cooks plan and prepare meals in private homes according to the client's tastes or dietary needs. They order groceries and supplies, clean the kitchen, and wash dishes and utensils. They also may serve meals. Personal chefs usually prepare a week's worth of meals in the client's home for the client to heat and serve according to directions. They may be self-employed or work as part of a team of personal chefs and employed by a company that provides this service. Private household cooks typically work full time for one client, such as corporate executives, university presidents, or diplomats, who regularly entertain as a part of their official duties (Bis, 2009).

Let me give you a case in point. Irena Chalmers, a well-known food jobs author, had one Korean culinary career student whose English-speaking ability did not quite match his exemplary cooking skills and found work as a private chef at the Korean

Embassy in Washington, D.C. The diplomats were delighted to have "home-cooked" food prepared by someone who spoke their language (For-your-dream-career, n.d.).

A freelance chef, or personal chef, does more than just cook in a client's home. He or she usually runs a business and must consider scheduling, planning, shopping, accounting and marketing. Some freelance chefs have assistants to help with food preparation and other tasks, but many freelancers work alone

Freelance chefs may also work in restaurants such as when the regular chef is on vacation. A freelance chef may even work for clients on yachts or help prepare food for a catering company. Being a freelance chef is not usually the same as being a caterer. Caterers often just prepare food for many different clients for parties and special occasions while freelance chefs tend to prepare food regularly for a handful of clients (Cyprus, n.d.).

⑦ Catering Chefs (Caterers and Event Planners, Catering Specialists) : Some Caterers own their own businesses, while others have managerial positions in hotel and resort catering operations. They provide services, food and beverages for various types of social functions. They design the perfect menus for a function or event, such as a wedding, company party, conference, intimate dinner or other type of social gatherings. Some caterers specialize in a specific type of food, while others specialize in foods for a specific type of event. Many catering chefs cross over the entire spectrum of styles in an effort to work in a variety of situations. They need to be able to produce large amounts of scrumptious food. They should also have good communication skills to collaborate on menus with their clients. Many catering chefs obtain certification through a culinary institute or technical school (Degreedirectory, n.d.; Baker, n.d.).

⑧ Food Stylists : They are responsible for the proper handling and preparation of food products for film, TV, and media, including understanding how to use food alternatives/substitutes, product sourcing, working with related industry contacts (photographers, prop stylists). A culinary background provides a foundation for recognizing good products, food color and texture balance, food traits and qualities (knowing what the product looks like raw, cooked, etc) (Frenchculinary, n.d.).

2) Career opportunities not involving cooking.

Not all positions of employment for culinary arts professionals involve cooking. Here are some examples.

① Restaurateurs (Restaurant Owners) : They own and manage a restaurant (dictionary.cambridge, n.d.).

② Food Writers (Cookbook Authors, Food Critics) : They establish a public contact with the public on food trends, chefs and restaurants. Many write for newspapers, magazines and some publish books. Notables in this field include Julia Child, Craig Claiborne and James Beard (Directoryofschools, n.d.).

③ Entrepreneurs : They develop their own business with examples including restaurants, bakeries, specialty food manufacture (chocolates, cheese etc) (Directoryofschools, n.d.).

④ Media Personalities : They deliver all the information and entertainment services based on culinary activities to the home.

⑤ Food Service Managers (Restaurant Managers) : They are responsible for the daily operations of restaurants and other establishments that prepare and serve meals and beverages to customers. Besides coordinating activities among various departments, such as kitchen, dining room, and banquet operations, food service managers ensure that customers are satisfied with their dining experience. In addition, they oversee the inventory and ordering of food, equipment, and supplies and arrange for the routine maintenance and upkeep of the restaurant's equipment and facilities. Managers are generally responsible for all administrative and human-resource functions of the business, including recruiting new employees and monitoring employee performance and training (Bis, 2009).

⑥ Food and Beverage Managers (Food and Beverage Supervisors, Wines & Spirits Specialists) : They manage all food and beverage outlets in hotels and other large establishments (Directoryofschools, n.d.).

⑦ Food and Beverage Controllers (Purchasing Agents) : They purchase and source ingredients in large hotels as well as manage the stores and stock control (Directoryofschools, n.d.).

⑧ Consultants (Food Consultants, Design specialists, Restaurant Designers, Kitchen Designers) : They works with restaurant owners in development of menus, layout and design of dining room and establishing kitchen protocols (Directoryofschools, n.d.).

⑨ Salespeople (Sales Representatives) : They introduce chefs and business owners to new products and are able to demonstrate the proper use at equipment. They may sell any range at products needed in the industry from various food products to equipment (Directoryofschools, n.d.).

⑩ Educators : They teach others how to cook and persue goals in culinary arts (Directoryofschools, n.d.).

⑪ Research & Development Directors (Research and Development Chefs, Menu Development Chefs, Recipe/Food Tester) : They develop new products for commercial manufacturers, manage test kitchens for publications or kitchens for restaurant chains or grocery chains (Directoryofschools, n.d.).

⑫ Culinologists : Culinology® is the blending of the culinary arts and the science of food. It is defined as "the collaboration between culinary expertise and food science and how this collaboration affects the food we prepare and serve for consumption. Culinologists are skilled chefs who are creating a new generation of exciting, high quality convenience food products (Smsu, 2010).

Note

- requisite : an important necessary thing
- acclaim : public approval and praise
- entail : to make something necessary, or to involve something
- oversee : to watch or organize a job or an activity to make certain that it is being done correctly
- platter : a large plate used for serving food or a meal with one type of food served on a large plate
- diplomat : an official whose job is to represent one country in another, and who usually works in an embassy
- occasion : a special or formal event
- function : an official ceremony or a formal social event, such as a party or a special meal, at which a lot of people are usually present

- intimate : having, or being likely to cause, a very close friendship or personal or sexual relationship
- gathering : a party or a meeting when many people come together as a group
- scrumptious : tasting extremely pleasant; delicious
- collaborate : to work with someone else for a special purpose
- prop stylist : the person responsible for providing the tableware, linens, flowers, etc
- trait : a particular characteristic that can produce a particular type of behaviour
- upkeep : the cost or process of keeping something, such as a building, in good condition
- administrative : relating to the arrangements and work which is needed to control the operation of a plan or organization
- recruit : to persuade someone to work for a company or become a new member of an organization, especially the army
- monitor : to watch and check a situation carefully for a period of time in order to discover something about it
- outlet : shop that is one of many owned by a particular company and that sells the goods which the company has produced
- source : to get something from a particular place
- protocol : the rules of correct or appropriate behavior of a group, organization, or profession

3. All about Chefs

1) Chefs vs Cooks

Dr. Nordstrom always emphasizes in his seminars the difference between a cook and a chef: the cook follows recipes whereas the chef understands principles and applies them (Lemke, 2009).

Consider the difference between a cook and a chef. A cook can expertly follow a recipe. He or she can gather the ingredients, measure them out, and mix them together to create a set menu. Moreover, he or she can do this with only minimal variance in the result time after time. But, a cook struggles in creating a new recipe, working with new ingredients, or trying to please a group of diners with tastes different than that to which he or she is accustomed. The cook lacks the foundational understanding necessary to break new culinary ground. The chef on the other hand does understand the foundations of food and cooking. He or she not only knows what all the ingredients in a recipe are, he or she also understands why those ingredients go together and how they interact. The chef can easily substitute ingredients, or use those ingredients in new ways to obtain different effects. Because the chef understands the foundations of cooking, the chef is not limited to a recipe that someone else has already created. Instead, the chef can create new recipes as needed to best suit the demands of the circumstances (Harmon, 2008).

A dictionary definition of a chef is a professional cook, especially the principal cook in a hotel or restaurant, and in the same dictionary a cook is defined as somebody who prepares and cooks food, usually as a job or in a particular way (Encarta, n.d.). In many ways, especially in terms of job responsibility and rank in the culinary industry, a chef is different from a cook.

First of all, a chef is usually a professional cook who has undergone a formal education and has received a 4-year bachelor's degree or a 2-year associate degree in a culinary college or a university. Most of the chefs in large establishments especially hotels, casino and full-services restaurants have obtained at least a 2-year associate degree.

In terms of job responsibility, a chef is responsible for directing the activities of other kitchen staffs such as a cook and food preparation workers, and makes the final decision in determining how the food should be cook and presented to the customers, takes charge in menu planning, recipe creation, food and supply ordering and some specific cooking duties such as a customized meal. is also responsible for some of the management work in an organization, may be required to do work such as marketing, finance, business planning, communication, purchasing, and some computer work, and needs leadership skill such as the ability to manage a group of cooks and kitchen staffs and communicate effectively with them.

On the other hand, a cook is ranked lower than a chef in the organization hierarchy, and is only responsible for all the kitchen duties such as day to day food preparation and all the cooking. Depending on the size of the facility or restaurant, the number of cooks varies and each cook is responsible for a different part of the menu or different type of food. For instance, there are fry cooks, vegetable cooks, fry cooks, pastry cooks, and grill cooks. There maybe only one chef in the facility that manages all of these cooks. A cook may not require an associate degree or a bachelor's degree to handle the job. Most of the cooks learn their trade either through apprenticeship or some culinary training in high school or a college. They are not required to handle the management work. Their work function is limited to the duties performed in the kitchen.

In short, there maybe some job overlapping between a chef and cook in some establishments that employs them. But overall, a chef typically has more training than a cook, including a culinary degree, and a chef is doing more than just cooking and preparing food (Chefcareerhelp, n.d.).

2) Culinarians

A dictionary definition of a culinarian is a person skilled in the preparation of food (Thefreedictionary, n.d.). ACF defines a culinarian as a person who is positioned in any one station in a food service operation, responsible for preparing and cooking sauces, cold foods, fish, soups and stocks, meats, vegetables, eggs and other food items (Acfchefs, 2009). Also according to an ACF's membership brochure, a culinarian is defined as an individual not involved in the management or supervision of staff, with a minimum of 6 months full time employment (Nwaacf, 2009).

3) Food Preparation Workers

Other than a chef and cook, there is also a distinct type of kitchen staff called food preparation worker who is the last kitchen staff in the hierarchy. He or she works under the supervision of chefs and cooks. They perform duties which require less culinary skills. For example, they may chop vegetables, prepare salads and prepare all the ingredients used by the chefs and cooks (Chefcareerhelp, n.d.).

4) Culinary Artists

Culinary artists aren't just cooks—they are responsible for skillfully preparing meals that are as pleasing to the palate as to the eye, and for preparing appealing and tasteful foods for a variety of customers in different establishments. Whether customers are dining at a fine cuisine restaurant or getting lunch to go at a delicatessen, their food was well prepared by an individual with a profession in this field. Increasingly they are required to have a knowledge of the science of food and an understanding of diet and nutrition.

A culinary artist is not responsible for making any painting or doing any performances but the person is responsible for making meals. A culinary artist can work either for recreation or as a professional (Collegeinfo, n.d.; Altiusdirectory, n.d.).

Note

- apply : to make use of something or use it for a practical purpose
- measure sth out : to weigh or measure a small amount of something from a larger amount of something
- variance : a change that occurs in something
- time after time : again and again; repeatedly
- accustomed : familiar with something
- hierarchy : a system in which people or things are arranged according to their importance
- apprenticeship : somebody being trained by a skilled professional in an art, craft, or trade
- overlapping : to coincide or correspond in part with something in time, function, or purpose, or make something coincide or correspond with something else
- supervision : a critical watching and directing (as of activities or a course of action)
- delicatessen : a small shop that sells high quality foods, such as types of cheese and cold cooked meat, which often come from other countries

4. Essential Culinary Terms

1) Food Pyramid

Figure 2-1 shows a diagrammatic proportional representation of human nutritional needs updated in 2005 by the U.S. Department of Agriculture to replace the previous food pyramid created in 1992. The "My Pyramid" icon has 6 panels representing grains; vegetables; fruits; milk; meat and beans; and fats, sugars, and salts. According to My Pyramid, the majority of servings should come from grains, followed closely by milk, then by vegetables and fruits. Meat and beans should be lean and varied. Fats, sugars, and salt should be consumed sparingly (Mosby's Medical Dictionary, 2009).

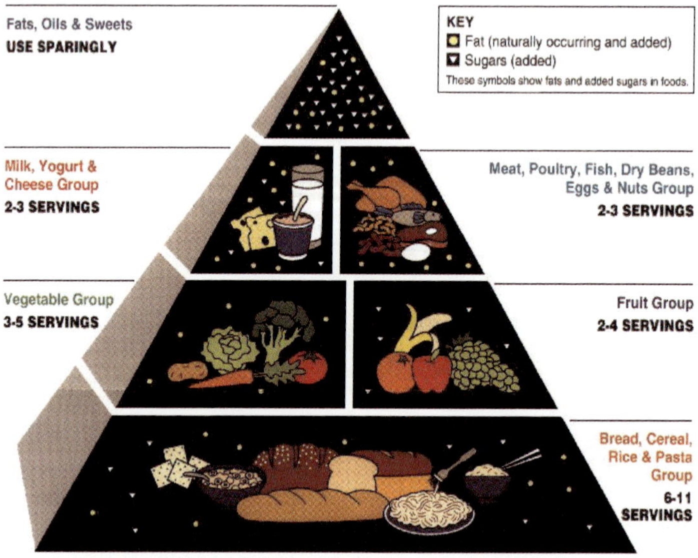

(source : http://medical-dictionary.thefreedictionary.com/food+pyramid)

Figure 2-1 Food pyramid

2) Organic foods

"Organic" refers not only to the food itself, but also to how it was produced. Foods labeled organic must meet or exceed the regulations of the National Organic Program (NOP), which took effect October 21, 2002. They must be grown and processed using organic farming methods that recycle resources and promote biodiversity. Crops must be grown without using synthetic pesticides, bioengineered genes, petroleum-based fertilizers and sewage sludge-based fertilizers. Organic livestock must have access to the outdoors and be given no antibiotics or growth hormones (FMI, 2007).

3) Mise en Place

Successful cooks and chefs all over the world apply a concept known as Mise en Place (MEEZ-ahn-plahs). The French definition means "everything in its place," and it is a culinary term that refers to preparing and pre-measuring ingredients ahead of time. However, Mise en Place is more than just a term; it is a concept or a state-of-mind that when applied to any kitchen, will result in a smooth-flowing, time saving cooking process. This is especially beneficial when preparing more than one recipe (Phytopia, n.d.).

4) Palate vs Texture

Palate is defined as a person's ability to taste and judge good food and wine(Dictionary.cambridge, n.d.), and texture is the feeling of the food in your mouth. In practice texture is not just one thing but lots of different sensations felt all at once.

Food scientists have tried to categorize different aspects of texture to understand what any item of food gives its particular feeling in our mouth. Here are some below (Eu-sol, n.d.):

① Juiciness — how much liquid is released when the food is crushed between molars?

② Firmness — how easy it is to squeeze?

③ Mealiness — how 'powdery' is the food e.g. cooked potato can be very mealy.

④ Toughness — how resistant the food is to puncture? This is similar to how easy is it to bite into.

⑤ Chewiness — how many chews does it take to reduce the food to a condition where it can be swallowed?

⑥ Elasticity — how much can the food be squeezed and still return to its original shape?

⑦ Meltiness — how quickly does the food dissolve in your mouth?

5) Aroma vs Smell vs Taste vs Flavor

Aroma is defined as a strong pleasant smell, usually from food or drink. Smell is defined the quality of something that can be detected by the sensitive nerves in the nose. Taste is defined as the sensation or perception of certain qualities of substances put in the mouth, primarily sweet, sour, salt and bitter. Flavor is defined as an identifiable or distinctive quality of food or drink perceived with the combined senses of taste and smell (Dictionary.cambridge, n.d.).

6) Taste buds

We taste with our 'taste buds'. If you look in a mirror you can see these; they are in the tiny bumps that are all over your tongue and the inside of your mouth. Taste buds are clumps of around 100 taste cells. These taste cells respond to types of chemicals and give rise to one of six tastes such as sweet, sour salty, bitter, and spicy and umami (or savory) (Eu-sol, n.d.).

7) Maillard reactions

The Maillard reaction is named after the French scientist Louis Camille Maillard (1878-1936), who studied the reactions of amino acids and carbohydrates in 1912, as part of his PhD thesis, which was published in 1913. The Maillard reaction is not a single reaction, but a complex series of reactions between amino acids and reducing sugars, usually at increased temperatures. Like caramelization, it is a form of non-enzymatic browning.

In the process, hundreds of different flavor compounds are created. These compounds in turn break down to form yet more new flavor compounds, and so on. Each type of food has a very distinctive set of flavor compounds that are formed during the Maillard reaction.

Maillard reactions are important in baking, frying or otherwise heating of nearly all foods. Maillard reactions are (partly) responsible for the flavor of bread, cookies, cakes, meat, beer, chocolate, popcorn, cooked rice. In many cases, such as in coffee, the flavor is a combination of Maillard reactions and caramelization. However, caramelization only takes place above 120-150 °C, whereas Maillard reactions already occur at room temperature.

Although studied for nearly one century, the Maillard reactions are so complex that still many reactions and pathways are unknown. Many different factors play a role in the Maillard formation and thus in the final colour and aroma; pH (acidity), types of amino acids and sugars, temperature, time, presence of oxygen, water, water activity (aw) and other food components all are important.

The Maillard reaction products thus change the colour and flavor of food, and in most cases these changes are appreciated by people. In addition the melanoidins may have some beneficial anti-oxidant properties.

On the other hand, Maillard reactions may reduce the nutritional value of a product, as amino acids and carbohydrates may be lost. Sometimes the flavour is not appreciated, such as the 'cooking flavor' in sterilized milk.

Some of the Maillard end-products may also be toxic or carcinogenic. One of the Maillard reaction products is acrylamide, a potential toxic compound which is only formed at temperatures above 180 °C, especially in baked or fried products (French fries). When frying below 180 °C acrylamide is not formed.

In general it can be stated that Maillard products have been present in our foods for many thousands of years, and are consumed daily by nearly all people in the world.

Maillard reactions can not, or hardly, be prevented when heating foods. Only by removing the sugars or the amino acids, or making the product very acid or alkaline, the reactions can be prevented (Food-info, n.d.).

8) Gourmet vs Foodie

Although the two terms are sometimes used interchangeably, foodies differ from gourmets in that gourmets are epicures of refined taste who may or may not be professionals in the culinary industry, whereas foodies are amateurs who simply love food for consumption, study, preparation, and news. Gourmets simply want to eat the best food, whereas foodies want to learn everything about food, both the best and the ordinary, and about the science, industry, and personalities surrounding food. For this reason, foodies are sometimes viewed as obsessively interested in all things culinary. There is also a general feeling in the culinary industry that the term gourmet is outdated (Gocalaverasfoodie, n.d.).

9) Decorate vs Garnish

The word decorate is defined as adding something to an object or place, especially in order to make it more attractive. The word garnish is defined as decorating food with a small amount of different food (Dictionary.cambridge, n.d.).

10) Vegan vs Vegetarian

The term vegan is a person who does not eat or use any animal products, such as meat, fish, eggs, cheese or leather. The term vegetarian is a person who does not eat meat for health or religious reasons or because they want to avoid being cruel to animals (Dictionary.cambridge, n.d.). Figure 2-2 shows vegan food guide as a daily plan for healthy eating.

11) N.R.A. (National Restaurant Association)

It was founded in 1919, the National Restaurant Association is the leading business association for the restaurant industry. Together with the National Restaurant Association Educational Foundation, its goal is to lead America's restaurant industry into a new era of prosperity, prominence, and participation, enhancing the quality of life for all we serve (Restaurant, n.d.).

(Source : http://runforawareness.ca/foodguide.htm

Figure 2-2 Vegan Food Guide (Daily Plan For Healthy Eating)

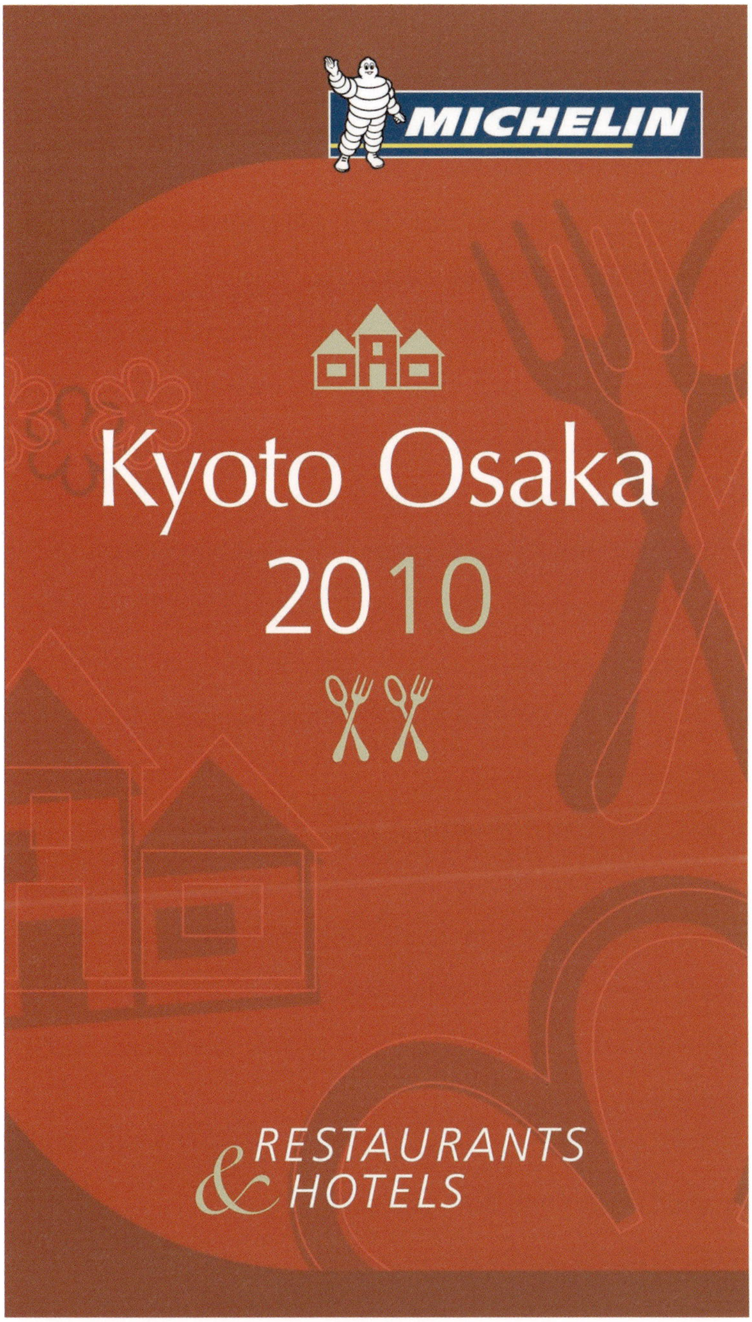

(Source : www.michelin.com.mx/Noticias/img/f/FP_11.jpg)

Figure 2-3 Cover of Michelin Guide Kyoto Osaka 2010

12) What is Michelin Guide?

① History of Michelin Guide

André Michelin published the first edition of the guide to help drivers maintain their cars, find decent lodging, and eat well while touring France. The guide was distributed freely from 1900 until 1920. The Michelin brothers introduced the charge to establish more credibility. The guide introduced the star in 1926 to note good cooking; two and three stars were added in the early 1930s. The cover of the guide was originally blue, but since 1931 has been red.

There are now Red Guides covering France, Austria, Netherlands, Belgium/ Luxembourg, Italy, Germany, Spain/Portugal, Switzerland, and the UK/Ireland. The first guides for cities outside of Europe were published in 2006 for New York City and for San Francisco. Guides for Tokyo, Los Angeles and Las Vegas have been released since November 2007. A guide for Hong Kong and Macau was published on 5 December 2008. A guide for Kyoto and Osaka was published on 16 October 2009. Kyoto and Osaka were awarded a total of 106 and 79 stars respectively.

A restaurant that receives one or more stars is not only one of the best in its city or country but also one of the best in the world. A 3-star Michelin ranking is exceedingly rare. Only 26 3-star restaurants exist in France, and only 81 in the world (Mackintoshs, n.d.; Fluccola, n.d.; Jnto, 2009; Motortrend, 2009).

② The Ratings

A very good restaurant in its category

Excellent cooking and worth a detour

Exceptional cuisine and worth the journey

The Michelin Guide uses a system of symbols to identify the best hotels and restaurants within each comfort and price category. For restaurants, Michelin stars are based on five criteria (Michelinguide, n.d.):

The quality of the products

The mastery of flavor and cooking

The "personality" of the cuisine

The value for the money

The consistency between visits

Michelin stars are awarded to restaurants offering the finest cooking, regardless of the country or type of cuisine. Stars represent only what is on the plate. They do not take into consideration interior decoration, service quality or table settings. Decisions to award stars are made collectively. All the inspectors who have evaluated a meal in a given restaurant present and support their opinions, based on their experiences and reports (Michelin, 2009).

Comfort is rated by fork-and-spoon symbols for restaurants. This is completely independent from the number of stars, and assesses the establishment's equipment such as exterior and interior, and service. For hotels, pavilion symbols indicate the comfort. In case of price they must have a menu priced at no more than £28 in the case of the UK (Motortrend, 2009; Michelin, 2009). (See Figure 2-3)

Note

- sparing : using very little of something
- take effect : to produce or achieve the results you want
- biodiversity : the number and types of plant and animal species that exist in a particular environmental area or in the world generally, or the problem of

protecting this

- synthetic : describes products that are made from artificial substances, often copying a natural product
- pesticide : a chemical substance used to kill harmful insects, small animals, wild plants and other unwanted organisms
- bioengineer : to modify or produce by bioengineering <bioengineered insulin>
- fertilizer : a natural or chemical substance which is spread on the land or given to plants, to make plants grow well
- sewage : waste matter such as water or human urine or solid waste
- sludge : soft wet soil or a substance that looks like this
- livestock : animals, such as cows and sheep, and birds, such as chickens, kept on a farm
- antibiotic : a medicine or chemical that can destroy harmful bacteria in the body or limit their growth
- molar : one of the large teeth at the back of the mouth in humans and some other animals used for crushing and chewing food
- mealy : dry and powdery
- puncture : to make a small hole in something, or to get a small hole in something
- bite into : to reduce something valuable
- bump : a round, raised area on a surface or on the body
- umami : a taste sensation that is meaty or savory and is produced by several amino acids and nucleotides
- savory : pleasing to the sense of taste especially by reason of effective seasoning
- thesis : a long piece of writing on a particular subject, especially one that is done for a higher college or university degree
- caramelize : to cook a food with sugar so that the food becomes sweet and often brown
- yet : used to add emphasis to words such as another and again, especially to show an increase in amount or the number of times something happens ex) He's given us yet more work to do.

- pathway : a sequence of biochemical reactions involved in a metabolic process
- melanoidin : any of various colored substances formed from proteins or amino acids (as in the presence of glucose)
- appreciate : to increase in value, especially over time
- sterilize : to make something completely clean and free from bacteria
- carcinogenic : describes a substance which causes cancer
- epicures : a person who enjoys food and drink of a high quality; a gourmet
- obsessive : thinking about something or someone, or doing something, too much or all the time
- outdated : old-fashioned and therefore not as good or as fashionable as something modern
- cruel : extremely unkind and unpleasant and causing pain to people or animals intentionally
- prominence : the condition or quality of being significantly important or well-known
- decent : socially acceptable or good
- charge : the amount of money that you have to pay for something, especially for an activity or service
- exceedingly : to a very great degree; extremely
- comfort : conditions in which somebody feels physically relaxed
- mastery : expert knowledge or outstanding ability
- personality : the distinguishing characteristics of a place or situation
- consistency : the ability to maintain a particular standard or repeat a particular task with minimal variation
- pavilion : one of a group of related buildings

References

Altiusdirectory, "CULINARY ARTS," Retrieved Jan. 13, 2010 from http://www.altiusdirectory.com/Arts/culinary-arts.html

Articlesbase, 2009, "Deciding to Start a New Career in the Culinary Arts," Dec. 18, Retrieved Jan. 14, 2010 from http://www.articlesbase.com/career-management-articles/deciding-to-start-a-new-career-in-the-culinary-arts-1597894.html,

Baker, "Caterer," Retrieved Jan. 14, 2010 from http://www.baker.edu/career-explorer/career/caterer/

Bis, 2009, "Food Service Managers Occupational Outlook Handbook," 2010-11 Edition, December 17, Retrieved Jan. 14, 2010 from http://www.bls.gov/oco/ocos024.htm

Careereducationadvisor, "Profile: Culinary Industry," Retrieved Jan. 14, 2010 from http://www.careereducationadvisor.com/Profile-Culinary-Industry.htm

Careers.collegetoolkit, "Chefs and Head Cooks," Retrieved Jan. 14, 2010 from http://careers.collegetoolkit.com/careers/chefs_and_head_cooks /tasks/35-1011.00.aspx

Chefcareerhelp, "What Is The Difference Between A Chef And A Cook?," Retrieved Jan. 14, 2010 from http://chefcareerhelp.com/types-of-chefs /what-is-the-difference-between-a-chef-and-a-cook/

Collegeinfo, "Cooking Up A Career: The Culinary Arts," Retrieved Jan. 13, 2010 from http://www.collegeinfo.com/cooking-up-a-career-the-culinary-arts

Cookingschools, "Executive Chef," Retrieved Jan. 14, 2010 from http://www.cookingschools.com/cooking-culinary-careers /executive-chef.html

Culinaryed, "Becoming a Skilled Chef." Retrieved Jan. 9, 2010 from http://www.culinaryed.com/

Cyprus, Sheri, "What is a Freelance Chef?," Retrieved Jan. 14, 2010 from http://www.wisegeek.com/what-is-a-freelance-chef.htm

Degreedirectory, "Catering Chef: Become a Catering Chef in 5 Steps," Retrieved Jan. 14, 2010 from http://degreedirectory.org/articles /Catering_Chef_Become_a_Catering_Chef_in_5_Steps.html

Directoryofschools, "Campus Programs," Retrieved Jan. 14, 2010 from http://www.directoryofschools.com/LEcole-Culinaire/Culinary-Arts.htm

Edu.chefsblade, "Cooking Career Specialties," Retrieved Jan. 14, 2010 from http://edu.chefsblade.com/v/main/articles /2331-cooking-career-specialties_cs

Eu-sol, "What is taste?/What is texture?," Retrieved Jan. 4, 2010 from http://www.eu-sol.net/

FMI(Food Marketing Institute), 2007, Natural and Organic Foods, Jun.,Retrieved Jan. 4, 2010 from http://www.fmi.org/media/bg/natural_organic_foods.pdf

Fluccola, "Did You know? - The story of Michelin Stars," Retrieved Jan. 4, 2010 from http://www.facebook.com/pages/Budapest/Fruccola /55449249461?v=app_2347471856

Food-info, "Maillard reactions," Retrieved Jan. 4, 2010 from http://www.food-info.net /uk/colour/maillard.htm

For-your-dream-career, "Food Jobs - For All Food Lovers," Retrieved Jan. 14, 2010 from http://www.for-your-dream-career.com/Food-Jobs.html

Frenchculinary, Careers outside of the kitchen, Retrieved Jan. 14, 2010 from http://www.frenchculinary.com/alumni_careers.htm

Gocalaverasfoodie, "What is a Foodie?," Retrieved Jan. 4, 2010 from http://gocalaverasfoodie.com/what-is-a-foodie/

Harmon, Stephen W., 2008, "A Theoretical Basis for Learning in Massive Multiplayer

Virtual Worlds," Journal of Educational Technology Development and Exchange, November, 2008, 1(1):29-40, Retrieved Jan. 14, 2010 from http://www.sicet.org/jetde/jetde08/paper03.pdf

Jnto, 2009, "Kyoto & Osaka - New Destinations for Gourmet Travellers," Japan National Tourism Organization, London Office, Press Release. 17, Sep, Retrieved Jan. 4, 2010 from http://www.seejapan.co.uk/contact/press/img/pdf /pr_09Sep17_travellers.pdf

Jwu, 2008, "College Of Culinary Arts," Retrieved Dec. 27, 2009 from http://www.jwu.edu/college.aspx?id=30742

Lemke, Ljuba, 2009, "ALF (Advanced Lightwire Functionals), Cranial Osteopathy, and Overall Health, Holistic," Health Source, April, Retrieved Jan. 14, 2010 from http://www.alforthodontics.com/ALF_CO_Health.pdf

Michelin, 2009, "MICHELIN guide Kyoto Osaka will be the second MICHELIN guide published in Japan," 4, Jun. Retrieved Jan. 4, 2010 from http://www.michelin.co.uk/michelinuk/en/more/news-detail/news /20080819113604/24789.html

Michelinguide, "The ratings," Retrieved Jan. 4, 2010 from http://www.michelinguide.com/us/ratings.html

Motortrend, 2009, "MICHELIN Guide Kyoto Osaka Will Be the Second MICHELIN Guide Published in Japan," Auto News, 6, Apr. Retrieved Jan. 4, 2010 from http://www.motortrend.com/features/newswire/42515/index.html

Newfuturesdc, 2009, 2009-2010 Career Guide; Promising Careers that Don't Require Four Years of College, New Futures, Retrieved Feb. 5, 2010 from http://www.newfuturesdc.org/wp-content/uploads/2009/11/Career-Guide.pdf

Nwaacf, 2009, "Newsletter: On the plate," Sep. Retrieved Jan. 14, 2010 from http://www.nwaacf.com/uploads/Sept_ACF_Newsletter1.pdf

Phytopia, "Mise en Place; Everything in its Place," Retrieved Jan. 5, 2010 from http://www.phytopia.com/newsletter/misenplace.htm.

Restaurant, "About the National Restaurant Association," Retrieved Jan. 4, 2010 from http://www.restaurant.org/aboutus/

Skillsalberta, 2009, "34 CULINARY ARTS," Retrieved Jan. 9, 2010 from http://www.skillsalberta.com/pdf/promomaterial/SchoolTours2.pdf

Smith, Anne Kates, 2009, "Seasoned to Taste: Culinary Industry Opportunities Come in Many Flavors," Jul. 26, Retrieved Jan. 14, 2010 from http://educo.uber.matchbin.net/printer_friendly/3035068

Smsu, "Culinology," 2010, Jan. 10, Retrieved Jan. 14, 2010 from http://www.smsu.edu/Academics/Programs/Culinology /Index.cfm?Id=795&output=pdf

Snider, Sue, 2007, "Using Herbs and Spices," 15, Mar., Retrieved Jan. 4, 2010 from http://ag.udel.edu/extension/fnutri/pdf/CookingGuide/fnf-03.pdf

Thefreedictionary, "culinarian," Retrieved Jan. 14, 2010 from http://www.thefreedictionary.com/Culinarian

Ufl, "Career Development," Retrieved Jan. 7, 2010 from http://www.law.ufl.edu /career/faqs/#8

The New Yorker, November 23, 2009, p. 44

Retrieved Jan. 13, 2010 from http://dictionary.cambridge.org/

Retrieved Jan. 13, 2010 from http://encarta.msn.com/

Retrieved Jan. 13, 2010 from http://www.merriam-webster.com/dictionary/

Retrieved Jan. 7, 2010 from http://dictionary.cambridge.org/

Chapter 03

Positive Attitude toward the Culinary Industry

Difference between Knowledge and Understanding

Knowledge

Understanding

KNOWLEDGE IS VITAL. BUT KNOWLEDGE IS NOTHING WITHOUT UNDERSTANDING.

(Source : http://www.doremus.com/pr/K_U%20wine.pdf)

Learn from your Past

Cultivate your Future!

1. The Professional Chef

1) A Poem from the Kitchen

I Am A Chef

Written by Jema Ema

I am a chef; every day I waked up tired.
I am a chef; every day my feet are sore.
I am a chef; every day I ride the bus with workers who will finish at five.
I am a chef; and today I will skip my break.
I am a chef; every day sweat stings my eyes.
I am a chef; every day I deal with bullshit.
I am a chef; every day I fight waiters.
I am a chef; I have scares to prove it.
I am a chef; every day I peel, chop, and slice.
I am a chef; every day I learn, teach, and create.
I am a chef; every day I reach a natural high.
I am a chef, and at the end of every day—I am proud of what I do...

(Source : Retrieved Jan. 10, 2004 from http://www.globalchefs.com/article/archive/art062iam.htm)

2) A True Chef

The term "chef," although frequently used to describe anyone who cooks, is considered a mark of respect by those within the profession. The title is one that can only be earned through diligent practice and dedication. Those chefs who have made, or will make, the most lasting impression on this industry know that their success depends on their ability to fulfill many different roles. A true chef is, among other things, a lifelong student, a teacher, a craftsman, a leader, and a manager. An open and inquiring mind, an appreciation of and dedication to quality and excellence, and a sense of responsibility to self and the community are among the professional chef's cardinal virtues (Donovan, 1996).

Note

- profession : a type of job that needs special training or skill, especially one that needs a high level of education
- dedication : the hard work and effort that sb puts into an activity or purpose because they think it is important: hard work and dedication
- chef : a professional cook, especially the most senior cook in a restaurant, hotel, etc.
- craftsman : a skilled person, especially one who makes beautiful things by hand
- appreciation : a full or sympathetic understanding of sth, such as a situation or a problem, and of what it involves
- community : all the people who live in a particular area, country, etc. when talked about as a group
- cardinal : most important; having other things based on it
- virtue : a particular good quality or habit

3) Professionalism

No matter what your co-worker's attitudes, your professionalism demonstrates to others a level of commitment and a personal focus on excellence. What does it mean to be a professional? Consider the following list (Larousse, 1996).

Elements of Professionalism

① Focus on the job at hand, and perform all tasks and responsibilities to the best of your ability.

② Wear clean and well-pressed proper attire, and maintain good personal hygiene.

③ Practice being a good listener. (This promotes teamwork, esprit de corps, and camaraderie.)

④ Avoid profanity, crude jokes, and gossip. No matter how tough things are, make an effort to accentuate the positive.

⑤ Remember, the culinary industry is a service industry. Customer-oriented service is the best advertising for any service business.

⑥ Learn to wind down after each work day by cultivating conversation with friends and co-workers, reading, and other constructive activities.

⑦ Establish a steadfast rule: Never consume alcohol during a work shift.

⑧ Physically demanding work does not take the place of healthful exercise. Set aside time weekly to maintain good physical fitness.

⑨ Do all things in moderation. (It takes 21 consecutive days to develop a new habit.)

⑩ Arrive at work punctually and stay until the last customer is served.

Not all kitchens adhere to guidelines like these. In every profession there are pockets of enlightenment and harmony, as well as places where personal biases and ego-driven personalities get in the way of a focus on excellence. All students of the culinary arts are encouraged to find a niche where their creativity can flower, and where co-workers consider the following important but simple guidelines as a valid communal affirmation to be adhered to by all:

Kitchen User's Guide

- If you open it, close it.
- If you get it out, put it away.
- If you turn it on, turn it off.
- If you move it, put it back.
- If you spill it, wipe it up.
- If you get it dirty, clean it up.
- you unlock it, lock it up.
- If you break it, get it fixed.
- If you care about it, treat it as your own.

Finally, if a question arises about who is responsible for what job, remember the story about Everybody, Somebody, Anybody, and Nobody:

There was an important job to be done, and Everybody was sure that Somebody would do it. Anybody could have done it, but Nobody did it. Somebody got angry about that, because it was Everybody's job. Everybody thought Anybody could do it, but Nobody realized that Everybody wouldn't do it. It ended up that Everybody blamed Somebody when Nobody did what Anybody could have done.

Note

- Professionalism : the high standard that you expect from a person who is well trained in a particular job

- attire : clothes
- maintain : to make sth continue at the same level, standard, etc.
- hygiene : the practice of keeping yourself and your living and working areas clean in order to prevent illness and disease
- esprit de corps : (from French) feelings of pride, care and support for each other, etc. that are shared by the members of a group
- camaraderie : a feeling of friendship and trust among people who work or spend a lot of time together
- profanity : swear words, or religious words used in a way that shows a lack of respect for God or holy things
- accentuate : to emphasize sth or make it more noticeable
- positive : a good or useful quality or aspect
- wind down : to rest or relax after a period of activity or excitement
- steadfast : not changing in your attitudes or aims
- set aside : to save or keep money or time for a particular purpose in moderation
- adhere to : to behave according to a particular law, rule, set of instructions, etc.; to follow a particular set of beliefs or a fixed way of doing sth
- profession : a type of job that needs special training or skill, especially one that needs a high level of education
- enlightenment : knowledge about and understanding of sth; the process of understanding sth or making sb understand it
- get in the way of : to prevent sb from doing sth; to prevent sth from happening
- communal : shared by, or for the use of, a number of people, especially people who live together

4) Standards of Professionalism

The emphasis of a food service education is on learning a set of skills. But in many ways, attitudes are more important than skills because a good attitude will help you not only learn skills but also persevere and overcome the many difficulties you will face in your career. The successful food service worker follows an unwritten code of behavior and set of attitudes we call professionalism. Let's look at some of the qualities that a professional must have (Larousse, 1996).

① Positive attitude toward the job

In order to be a good professional cook, you have to like cooking and want to do it well. Being serious about your work doesn't mean you can't enjoy it. But the enjoyment comes from the satisfaction of doing your job well and making everything run smoothly.

Every experienced chef knows the stimulation of the rush. When it's the busiest time of the evening, the orders are coming in so fast you can hardly keep track of them, and every split second counts—then, when everyone digs in and works together and everything clicks, there's real excitement in the air. But this excitement comes only when you work for it.

A cook with a positive attitude works quickly, efficiently, neatly, and safely. Professionals have pride in their work and want to make sure that the work is something to be proud of.

② Staying power

Food service requires physical and mental stamina, good health, and a willingness to work hard. It is hard work. The pressures can be intense and the hours long and grueling. You may be working evenings and weekends when everyone else is playing. And the work can be monotonous. You might think it's drudgery to hand-shape two or three dozen dinner rolls for your baking class, but wait until you get that job in the big hotel and are told to make 3000 canapés for a party.

③ Ability to work with people

Few of you will work in an establishment so small that you are the only person on the staff. Food service work is teamwork, and it's essential to be able to work well on a team and to cooperate with your fellow workers. You can't afford to let ego problems, petty jealousy, departmental rivalries, or feelings about other people get in the way of doing the job well. In the old days, many chefs were famous for their temper tantrums. Fortunately, self-control is more valued today.

④ Eagerness to learn

There is more to learn about cooking than you will learn in a lifetime. But isn't it great to try? The greatest chefs in the world are the first to admit that they have more to learn, and they keep working, experimenting, and studying.

The food service industry is changing so rapidly that it is vital to be open to new ideas. No matter how good your techniques are, you might learn an even better way.

⑤ A full range of skills

Most people who become professional cooks do so because they like to cook. This is an important motivation, but it is also important to develop and maintain other skills that are necessary for the profession. To be successful, a cook must understand and manage food cost and other financial matters, manage and maintain proper inventories, deal with purveyors, and understand personnel management.

⑥ Experience

One of the most respected chefs has said, "You don't really know how to cook a dish until you have done it a thousand times."

There is no substitute for years of experience. Studying cooking principles in books and in schools can get your career off to a running start. You may learn more about basic cooking theories from your chef instructors than you could in several years of working your way up from washing vegetables. But if you want to become an accomplished cook, you need practice, practice, and more practice. A diploma will not make you a chef.

⑦ Dedication to quality

Many people think that only a special category of food can be called gourmet food. It's hard to say exactly what that is. Apparently, the only thing so-called gourmet foods have in common is high price.

The only distinction worth making is between well-prepared food and poorly prepared food. There is good roast duckling à l'orange and there is bad roast duckling à l'orange. There are good hamburgers and French fries, and there are bad hamburgers and French fries.

you work in a fancy French restaurant, a fast-food restaurant, a college cafeteria, or a catering house, you can do your job well, or not. The choice is yours.

High quality doesn't necessarily mean high price. It costs no more to cook green beans properly than to overcook them. But in order to produce high-quality food, you must want to. It is not enough to know how.

⑧ Good understanding of the basics

Experimentation and innovation in cooking are the order of the day. Brilliant chefs are breaking old boundaries, inventing dishes that would have been unthinkable years ago. There seems to be no limit to what can be tried.

However, the very chefs who seem to be most revolutionary are the first to insist on the important of solid grounding in basic techniques and in the classic methods practiced since Escoffier's day. In order to innovate, you have to know where to begin.

For the beginner, knowing the basics will help you take better advantage of your experience. When you watch a practiced cook at work, you will understand better what you are seeing and will know what questions to ask. In order to play great music on the piano, you first have to learn to play scales and exercises.

Note

- persevere : to try to do or continue doing something in a determined way, despite difficulties
- overcome : To prevail over; surmount
- face : To confront with complete awareness
- career : A chosen pursuit; a profession or occupation
- code : A systematic collection of regulations and rules of procedure or conduct
- rush : General haste or busyness
- keep track : If you keep track, you make certain that you know what is happening or has happened to someone or something.
- split : being divided or separated
- count : to have value or importance; to matter
- dig in : To begin to work intensively
- click : To function well together; hit it off
- in the air : prevalent
- grueling : extremely tiring and difficult, and demanding great effort and determination
- drudgery : hard monotonous routine work
- canapé : An appetizer prepared on a base such as toast or crackers.
- staff : the group of people who work for an organization
- cooperate : work together on a common enterprise or project

- ego : An exaggerated sense of self-importance; conceit
- petty : Of small importance; trivial
- jealousy : a feeling of jealous envy (especially of a rival)
- in the way : In a position to obstruct, hinder, or interfere
- temper : the usual state of your feelings which makes you become angry easily or stay calm
- tantrum : a sudden period of uncontrolled childish anger
- inventory : a detailed list of all the items in a place
- deal with : to take action on; to manage
- purveyor : someone who supplies provisions (especially food)
- substitute : One that takes the place of another; a replacement
- get off to : to start to do something in a particular way
- running start : A quick or auspicious beginning
- gourmet : a person who knows a lot about food and cooking, and who enjoys eating high-quality food
- duckling : young duck
- à l'orange : with orange glaze and/or sauce
- grounding : an area of knowledge or experience; a subject
- innovate : to introduce changes and new ideas
- practiced : skillful after much practice
- scale : a set of notes played or sung in order, going up or down
- exercises : Exercises are a ceremony which includes speeches and usually traditional music or activities

5) The Four P's

This is based upon an article introduced on homepage of L'Academie de Cuisine which was retrieved on January 5, 2002. Let's look at it. Utilizing its well-honed programs of instruction, the L'Academie de Cuisine staff trains its students in basic and advanced techniques that focus on food purchasing, preparation, presentation and the development of a refined palate. These "Four P's" prepare our students to take their place alongside the great chefs of America (Lacademie, n.d.)

① Purchasing

Fine food requires quality raw materials, and the students at L'Academie learn the many purchasing skills necessary to locate and acquire these products. Instruction includes how to select only the freshest, highest quality ingredients while maintaining cost effectiveness. The one-year Culinary Career Training Program also instructs its students in the many facets of running a professional kitchen. Course work features training in kitchen management, ownership and operation, accounting and math principles for kitchen management.

② Preparation

From the first day in class, students begin learning the art of fine food preparation utilizing the proven classic techniques of French cuisine.

The staff of trained culinary professionals at L'Academie instructs students in these classic techniques and how to apply and adapt them to all international cuisines.

Students quickly are producing quality fine food as they build their knowledge of knife skills, basic to advanced cooking techniques and product preparation.

③ Presentation

Food must not only taste wonderful, but also be visually appealing. Through intensive theoretical and practical instruction, L'Academie students learn how to take raw ingredients and create a work of art that not only complements the flavors of the food, but makes it visually exciting.

This portion of the students' training is strengthened by their "hands-on" externship training. This integral part of the programs allow students to apply their classroom knowledge, hone their technical skills and begin developing their own style and creativity in a professional environment.

④ Palate

A refined palate is an integral part of becoming a successful culinary professional, but it is a process that takes time. L'Academie immediately helps students begin developing their palate through instruction in combining flavors and textures to create perfectly balanced foods. Future experience and discipline will allow students to acquire a discerning palate that is the difference between a good cook and a great cook.

Note

- presentation : the way in which sth is offered, shown, explained, etc. to others
- refined : polite, well educated and able to judge the quality of things
- palate : the ability to recognize and/or enjoy good food and drink
- ownership : the fact of owning sth
- hands-on : doing sth rather than just talking about it
- externship : See Section 2 in Chapter 7
- integral : being an essential part of sth
- discipline : an area of knowledge; a subject that people study or are taught, especially in a university
- discerning : able to show good judgement about the quality of sb/sth

2. Uniform

1) History

This professional attire is the outcome of gradual evolution and became completely standardized only in this century.

In medieval kitchens, cooks wore a variety of costumes. The only common denominator was the apron. By Victorian times, portraits reveal chefs and ordinary cuisiniers in white clothing. Chefs de partie generally are shown wearing white caps. Carême is credited with having introduced to Britain the toque or high, starched hat, which superseded the "night cap" type. Alfred Suzanne, in his book La Cuisine Anglaise (1894), gives 1840 as the year when the toque began to achieve popularity. But even after that, as great a chef as Alexis Soyer wore a tasseled black beret instead of the toque.

In Great Britain, a similar black skullcap is still worn by the master cook (the equivalent of the maître chef de cuisine) at the famous English-style restaurant Simpson's in the Strand. However, the darker, closer-fitting cap, even though it conveys effectively the prestige of top rank in the kitchen, is less cool and comfortable for working at the stove than the airy toque (Fuller, Knight, and Salter, 1985).

Note

- medieval : connected with the Middle Ages (about AD 1000 to AD 1450)
- Chefs de partie : known as station chef; produces the menu items under the direct supervision of the chef or sous-chef

- cuisinier : cook
- costume : the clothes worn by people from a particular place or during a particular historical period
- denominator : the number below the line in a fraction showing how many parts the whole is divided into
- credit : to believe or say that sb is responsible for doing sth, especially sth good
- toque : the tall white hat worn by chefs
- supersede : often passive] to take the place of sth/sb that is considered to be old-fashioned or no longer the best available
- tasseled : decorated with tassels
- skullcap : a small round cap worn on top of the head, especially by Jewish men and Catholic bishops
- equivalent : equal in value, amount, meaning, importance, etc
- chef de cuisine : known simply as chef; the person responsible for all kitchen operations, developing menu items and setting the kitchen's tone and tempo
- prestige : the respect and admiration that sb/sth has because of their social position, or what they have done

2) Styles

In addition to outward garments, underclothing and socks should be selected with care. In some warmer sections of the kitchen, physical activity causes considerable perspiration. A generous number of undergarments of an absorbent material such as cotton are therefore essential. Undergarments and socks should be changed daily. It is equally important to wear sound shoes that are in a good state of repair; bad footwear leads to tripping and accidents, as well as to discomfort and poor hygiene (Fuller, Knight, and Salter, 1985).

Note

- garment : a piece of clothing
- perspiration : drops of liquid that form on your skin when you are hot
- generous : more than is necessary; large
- absorbent : able to take in sth easily, especially liquid
- sound : in good condition; not damaged, hurt, etc
- footwear : anything that people wear on their feet, for example shoes and boots

3) The Role of the Uniform

There is a standard of dress for professionals working in a kitchen that has come to be accepted by both the profession and the public. The white jacket, tall hat (known as a toque blanche), apron, side towel, are all part of the image. Pants (typically a houndstooth check in this country, solid black in European countries), hard shoes, and a neckerchief all are considered important elements as well. Its distinctiveness and recognizability confer prestige and status. It should be carefully maintained and worn with pride. More than simply completing the "look" of the chef, these parts of the typical uniform have important roles to play in keeping workers safe as they work in what is a potentially dangerous (some might say hostile) environment (Donovan, 1996).

① The Hat

Escoffier wore a black beret, and Gordon Sinclair wears a baseball cap. Most chefs in this country and throughout the world have adopted a tall, chimney-like hat. The idea is to help contain the chef's hair, preventing it from falling into the food. There may be some absorption of sweat from overheated brows as well. The hat should be laundered regularly whether it is obviously dirty or not. Disposable caps of paper or some other inexpensive material are worth considering for reasons of hygiene and economy.

② The Neck Cloth(=Neckerchief)

There are many modes of tying and wearing the neck cloth. The original purpose of this appendage was to absorb facial perspiration, but the trend now is toward wearing it as a close-fitting, neatly knotted tie. No doubt this has occurred because kitchen heat is less intense than it was in the old days of open fires.

③ The Jacket and Pants

A sparkling clean jacket does more than give the chef a crisp professional look. More than simply completing the look of the chef, the parts of the typical chef's uniform play important roles in keeping workers safe as they operate in a potentially dangerous environment. The chef's jacket, for instance, is double-breasted, which creates a two-layer cloth barrier between the chest area and steam burns, splashes, and spills. The double-breasted design also means that the jacket can easily be rebuttoned on the opposite side to cover any spills. The sleeves of the jacket are long and should be worn long, not rolled up, to cover as much of the arm as possible in order to protect against burns and scalding splashes.

The same is true of pants. Shorts, while they may seem like a good idea for such a hot environment, are inappropriate, offering no protection from hot stoves, accidental encounters with steam kettles, and splashes from sloshing pots of stock or pasta water. Pants should be worn without cuffs, which can trap hot liquids and debris. Ideally, pants should have a snap fly and be worn without a belt; in case hot grease is spilled on the legs, this allows for extremely fast removal of the pants, which could lessen the severity of the burn.

④ Apron and Side Towels

The apron is worn to protect the jacket and pants from excessive staining. It should be clean at the start of the shift and, if necessary, should be changed during the course of a working shift. The same is true of side towels. Most chefs use side towels to protect their hands when working with hot pans, dishes, or other equipment. They are not meant to be used as wiping cloths. If you do use a side towel to clean up a spill or wipe off a cutting board, replace it with a clean one.

Side towels used to lift hot items must be dry in order to provide protection. Once they become even slightly wet, they can no longer insulate your hands; the heat passes through the wet cloth quickly. If, like most people, you react by dropping the pan or pot, it is likely that you will wind up with even more burns, from the hot food that splashes on your legs and feet.

⑤ Shoes

While athletic shoes are very comfortable, they are not ideal for working in a kitchen. If a knife or other sharp object should fall from a work surface onto your feet, most athletic shoes would offer very little resistance, and you would wind up with a puncture wound. Hard leather shoes with slip-resistant soles are recommended, both because of the protection they offer from knives and because of the support they can give to your feet. A job that involves standing for several hours at a time puts a premium on good-quality, supportive, protective footgear.

There are several brands available, and it is worth the time and trouble to try on several different types of shoes to determine which are most suitable for you. Neglecting your feet is a bad business, one that will pay you back with foot trouble, back pain, and discomfort throughout your life. If you develop trouble with your feet, seek professional help, consider orthotics, and carefully heed advice about what shoes and other devices are best for your particular needs.

Note

- houndstooth check : A textile design of small broken checks.
- hostile : making it difficult for sth to happen or to be achieved
- economy : the use of the time, money, etc. that is available in a way that avoids waste
- appendage : a smaller or less important part of sth larger
- sparkling : shining and flashing with light
- crisp : pleasantly clear and sharp
- scalding : hot enough
- slosh : to move around making a lot of noise or coming out over the edge of sth
- snap fly : 스냅 지퍼(단추)
- insulate : to protect sth with a material that prevents heat, sound, electricity, etc. from passing through
- wind up : to bring sth such as a speech or meeting to an end
- footgear : Sturdy footwear, such as shoes or boots.
- orthotics : The science that deals with the use of specialized mechanical devices to support or supplement weakened or abnormal joints or limbs.
- heed : to pay careful attention to sb's advice or warning

3. Lab Requirements and Uniform & Personal Hygiene Code

This is part of a syllabus for culinary arts used in a community college in the United States. It is a typical example of uniform and personal hygiene code and lab requirements. You must follow these code and requirements just after this course. Let's explore it (Houston Community College, n.d.).

1) Lab Requirements

- Students are expected to attend class in chef uniform. The uniform consists of a chef jacket, chef checkered pants and a chef hat. Black leather shoes made with safety soles to prevent slipping.
- The students do not bring any tools to the classroom.
- For sanitary reasons, the students can only take notes on a pocket size notebook in class.

2) Uniform & Personal Hygiene Code

Everyone in the culinary field needs to be acutely aware of the need for good personal hygiene and sound sanitary practices in the preparation and handling of food. In order to establish consistent standards the HCC policy is as follows:

BEHAVIOR : sound hygienic practices must be demonstrated at all times. Failure to do so will result in a student being barred from class participation and possibly dropped from the program.

HAIR : must be neatly maintained, clean and under control at all times. A white bean cap is to be worn at all times. Male students must be clean-shaven. Beards and mustaches are permitted but must be clean and neatly trimmed.

HANDS : nails must be clean no artificial nails allowed, free of polish and cut short at all times. Wedding bands are the only permitted rings. Hands must always be washed at the beginning of each class and as needed during the day.

UNIFORMS : students are expected to wear a clean uniform daily consisting of a white chef's coat and black and white checkered pants and a white chef's hat.

SHOES : students are required to wear solid leather, black shoes with Non-skid soles and socks at all time. Students are expected to have purchased and be wearing complete uniforms by the first class meeting for baking class and fifth class meeting for culinary class.

Note

- hygiene : the degree to which people keep themselves or their environment clean, especially to prevent disease
- code : a set of principles that are accepted and used by society or a particular group of people
- laboratory : (informal lab) a room or place with appropriate equipment for teaching science or doing scientific work
- syllabus : (a plan showing) the subjects or books to be studied in a particular course, especially a course which leads to an examination
- checkered : patterned with alternating squares of color
- sole : the bottom part of a foot which touches the ground when you stand or walk, or the bottom part of a shoe which touches the ground, usually not including the heel
- sanitary : clean and not dangerous for the health, or protecting health by the removal of dirt and waste, especially human waste
- acutely : completely or extremely
- sound : showing good judgment; able to be trusted
- polish : a substance used to make something smooth or shiny
- wedding band : US for a wedding ring

References

Donovan, Mary Deirdre(ed.), 1996, The New Professional Chef, 6th ed.(New York: John Wiley & Sons, Inc.), p.11. pp.42～43.

Fuller, John, John B. Knight, and Charles A. Salter, 1985, Guide to Kitchen Management, (New York: VNR), pp.11～13.

Larousse, David Paul, 1996, The Professional Garde Manger(New York: John Wiley & Sons, Inc.), pp.19～20.

Retrieved Jan. 5, 2002 from http://www.globalchefs.com/article

Retrieved Jan. 5, 2002 from http://www.lacademie.com/pages/four_ps.html

Retrieved Jan. 13, 2002 from http://dictionary.cambridge.org/

Retrieved Jan. 6, 2002 from http://encarta.msn.com/encnet/features/dictionary/

Retrieved Jan. 5, 2002 from http://www.merriam-webster.com/dictionary/

Houston Community College, Syllabus, Retrieved Feb. 6, 2010 from http://www.hccs.edu/hcc/System%20Home/Departments/Workforce/Culinary%20Arts/pdf/pstr1340.pdf

Retrieved Feb. 6, 2010 from http://encarta.msn.com/

Retrieved Feb. 6, 2010 from http://www.merriam-webster.com/dictionary/

Retrieved Feb. 6, 2010 from http://dictionary.cambridge.org/

Chapter 04

New Phenomena and New Concepts

Think smart / Learn smart / Study smart

1. Slow Food

① Origin of Slow food

The slow food movement began in Italy in reaction to the opening of the first Italian McDonald's at the Spanish Steps in Rome. Seeing this as a threat to the traditional Italian culinary heritage, a group of activists, lead by Carlo Petrini, established slow food principles in 1986. Slow Food, the organization, was created in 1989 in Paris, taking the snail as its primary symbol (See Figure 4-1).

(Source : http://www.greenregion.eu/)

Figure 4-1 Slow Food Symbol Snail

More than half of the organization's membership is in Italy, but the organization boasts more than 100,000 members in 132 countries, including the United States, which claims 1,000 local chapters(convivia). There are currently chapters in Washington, D.C., New York City, Los Angeles and New Orleans, and also in smaller places like Fargo, North Dakota and Small Green Island, Washington (Matsey, 2003; Davey, 2004; SlowFoodbeirut, 2010; SlowFood, 2010) (See Figure 4-2).

② Philosophy of Slow food

We believe that everyone has a fundamental right to pleasure and consequently the responsibility to protect the heritage of food, tradition and culture that make this pleasure possible. Our movement is founded upon this concept of eco-gastronomy — a recognition of the strong connections between plate and planet.

Slow Food is good, clean and fair food. We believe that the food we eat should taste good; that it should be produced in a clean way that does not harm the environment, animal welfare or our health; and that food producers should receive fair compensation for their work.

We consider ourselves co-producers, not consumers, because by being informed about how our food is produced and actively supporting those who produce it, we become a part of and a partner in the production process (SlowFood, 2010).

② Mission of Slow food

Slow Food works to defend biodiversity in our food supply, spread taste education and connect producers of excellent foods with co-producers through events and initiatives (SlowFood, 2010) (See Figure 4-2).

■ Defence of Biodiversity

Slow Food believes the enjoyment of excellent food and drink should be combined with efforts to save the countless traditional grains, vegetables, fruits, animal breeds and food products that are disappearing due to the prevalence of convenience food and industrial agribusiness. Through the Ark of Taste and Presidia project (supported by the Slow Food Foundation for Biodiversity) and Terra Madre, Slow Food seeks to protect our invaluable food heritage.

■ Taste Education

By reawakening and training their senses, Slow Food helps people rediscover the joys of eating and understand the importance of caring where their food comes from, who makes it and how it's made. Convivium activities introduce local foods and producers to both members and non-members, while Taste Workshops offer guided tastings with food experts. School initiatives like convivium school gardens offer our youngest eaters hands-on learning experiences about the food they eat and grow themselves.

Slow Food created the University of Gastronomic Science to offer a multidisciplinary academic program in the science and culture of food. UNISG is another way in which Slow Food brings together the innovations and research of the academic and scientific world and the traditional knowledge of farmers and food producers.

■ Linking Producers and Co-producers

Slow Food organizes fairs, markets and events locally and internationally to showcase products of excellent gastronomic quality and to offer discerning consumers the opportunity to meet producers.

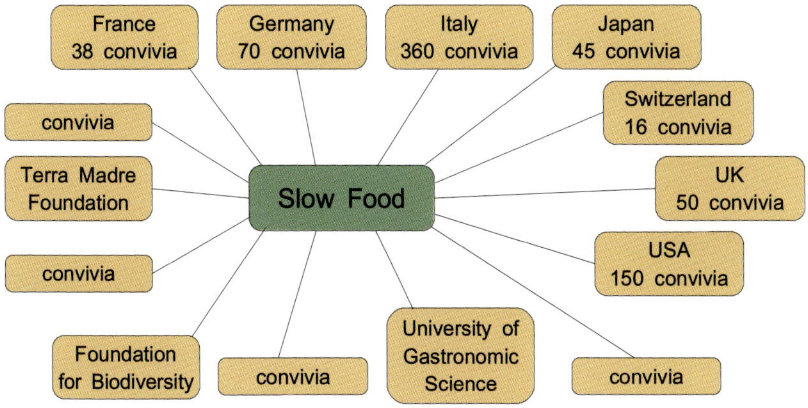

Source : Last updated April 2008. Accessed Jan. 3. 2010.
http://222.slowfoodeastbay.com/pdf/Companion08_ENG.pdf

Figure 4-2 Entire Slow Food Network

③ Embracing Slow Food By Joshna Maharaj

Joshna Maharaj is a busy chef with big ideas. With a simple but thoughtful approach to food and cooking, Joshna has embraced her new position as chef at Food Studio in the Royal Ontario Museum with excitement and enthusiasm. She is also a member of Slow Food and is constantly engaged with ideas about a truly sustainable food system and culture (Maharaj, 2009).

Whenever I tell people about Slow Food, they don't always get what I'm saying immediately. There are lots of questions about whether it's an organization promoting lengthy cooking times (and, therefore, eating only stews and braises) or chewing many times (slowly) before swallowing. But when I explain Slow Food is about standing in opposition to the values of fast food, I am almost instantly understood and people are curious to know more.

Slow Food was founded 20 years ago in 1989, to "counteract fast food and fast life, the disappearance of local food traditions and people's dwindling interest in the food they eat, where it comes from, how it tastes and how their food choices affect the rest of the world." To do this, Slow Food brings pleasure and responsibility together, giving them equal importance.

At the helm of this growing global movement is Carlo Petrini. Slow Food's founder, Petrini is an engaging and charismatic speaker with a serious passion for food and justice. He is supported by a number of "foodie" heavyweights around the world, including revolutionary American chef Alice Waters, food journalist Michael Pollan and global activist Vandana Shiva, to name a few.

For cooks around the world, embracing Slow Food can mean something as simple as preserving the traditions of the kitchen table. But for those who work in the hospitality industry, Slow Food values provide an incredible opportunity to connect with people in the community and provide leadership with regards to the sourcing of ingredients and the role food can play in people's lives.

Whether feeding kids at school, diners in a restaurant or delegates at a conference centre, chefs can incorporate Slow Food values into their kitchen in a few ways.

Perhaps the easiest is making a commitment to sourcing some food ingredients from local producers. Visit a farmer's market or ask a wholesaler to make connections with local farms for seasonal produce. Following from this, restaurant menus can reflect the bounty of the harvest, offering diners the delight of eating with the seasons.

Cooking good, wholesome food is the next step in this process. These days, people's busy lives find them outside of the home for many meals, relying on chefs and food service providers for much of their daily eating. Why not honour that need by offering nourishing, wholesome food to people instead of simply producing a plateful of half-hearted calories to gulp down. With beautiful, whole ingredients, even the simplest of preparations will result in a stellar plate, which will undoubtedly keep people coming back for more.

A third step in embracing Slow Food values involves the spirit and management of a restaurant kitchen. Having staff who are passionate about food and let that passion shine through their work is an invaluable asset. When there is an air of hospitality and positivity in a kitchen, people working in it thrive and that positivity undoubtedly makes its way to guests. Some of the earliest forms of human civilization involved gathering around a hearth to share food. Infusing service, both front and back of house, with this spirit of true hospitality is a profound way to reconnect people to this history.

Every kitchen, regardless of status or context, can nurture Slow Food values and make important links between producers and consumers. And in the effort to reconnect people with good, wholesome food, every little bit counts.

Note

- A convivium is a group of Slow Food members (minimum 20 people) in a particular region that supports the mission and guiding values of Slow Food, organizes events, and educates members. It is also the grass roots expression of the movement and a tool for implementing the Slow Food mission on a local level.

Convivia are chapters of Slow Food that form the foundation of conviviality and provide the grassroots fuel for the movement. Convivia are led by volunteer leaders, and a convivium is distinct in its approach and local activity. A convivium comes from the Latin word convivere — "to live with, hence to feast with"— because conviviality is an essential ingredient of Slow Food.

- gastronomy : gastronomy
- compensation : something that makes you feel better when you have suffered something bad
- biodiversity : the number and types of plant and animal species that exist in a particular environmental area or in the world generally, or the problem of protecting this
- initiative : a new action or movement, often intended to solve a problem
- prevalence : existing very commonly or happening often
- agribusiness : the various businesses that are connected with producing, preparing and selling farm products
- The Ark of Taste project : It aims to rediscover, catalog, describe and publicize forgotten flavors. It is a metaphorical recipient of excellent gastronomic products that are threatened by industrial standardization, hygiene laws, the regulations of large-scale distribution and environmental damage.
- Presidia project : The Presidia sustain quality production at risk of extinction, protect unique regions and ecosystems, recover traditional processing methods, safeguard native breeds and local plant varieties.
- Slow Food Foundation for Biodiversity : This is part of Slow Food and was founded in Florence in 2003 in partnership with the Tuscany Regional Authority. While it supports projects around the world, its most significant commitment is focused on developing countries, where defending biodiversity not only means improving people's quality of life, but can mean guaranteeing life itself.
- Terra Madre(The Food Communities Network) : Terra Madre brings together those players in the food chain who together support sustainable agriculture, fishing, and breeding with the goal of preserving taste and biodiversity.

- hands-on(PRACTICAL EXPERIENCE) : Someone who has hands-on experience of something has done or used it rather than just read or learned about it
- showcase : to show the best qualities or parts of something
- discerning : showing good judgment, especially about style and quality
- embrace : to accept something enthusiastically
- counteract : to reduce or remove the effect of something unwanted by producing an opposite effect
- dwindling : gradually decreasing until little remains
- helm : the handle or wheel which controls the direction in which a ship or boat travels
- engaging : pleasant, attractive and charming
- charismatic : describes a person who has charisma
- foodie : a person who loves food and is very interested in different types of food
- heavyweight : a person or thing that is important or serious and that other people notice
- with regards to something or someone : concerning someone or something
- source : to get something from a particular place
- incorporate : to include something as part of something larger
- bounty : a large amount
- wholesome : good for you, and likely to improve your life either physically, morally or emotionally
- honour : to show great respect for someone or something, especially in public
- half-hearted : showing no enthusiasm and interest
- gulp down : to eat or drink food or liquid quickly by swallowing it in large amounts, or to make a swallowing movement because of fear, surprise or excitement (often followed by down)
- stellar : of a star or stars
- hearth : the area around a fireplace or the area of floor in front of it
- infuse : to fill someone or something with an emotion or quality
- context : the situation within which something exists or happens, and that can help explain it
- count : to have value or importance; to matter

2. Molecular Gastronomy

① Origin and Definition of Molecular gastronomy

Today, molecular gastronomy has many names such as culinary alchemy, avant-garde cooking, scientific cooking, scientific cuisine, progressive cooking, experimental cuisine, and molecular cooking, etc (Yek & Struwe, 2008). It is known as "분자요리" or "분자요리학" in Korean (See Figure 4-3).

(Source : http://en.wikipedia.org/wiki/File:Raw_egg.jpg)

Figure 4-3 Molecular gastronomy includes the study of how different cooking temperatures affect eggs

Molecular gastronomy was born in 1988, when two scientists, Nicholas Kurti and Hervé This, created a new scientific discipline to investigate culinary transformations, specifically the chemistry and physics behind the preparation of food (This, 2006).

It is defined as a scientific discipline that studies the physical and chemical processes that occur while cooking (This, 2006). Molecular gastronomy seeks to investigate and explain the chemical reasons behind the transformation of ingredients, as well as the social, artistic and technical components of culinary and gastronomic phenomena in general (Wikipedia, 2010).

② Five aims of Molecular gastronomy

When Hervé This presented his Ph.D. dissertation "Molecular and Physical Gastronomy" at the University of Paris in 1996, he identified five aims of this new science:

- to collect and investigate old wives' tales about cooking
- to model and scrutinize existing recipes
- to introduce new tools, products, and methods to cooking
- to invent new dishes using knowledge from the previous three aims
- to use the appeal of food to promote science (This, 2005).

The first two aims are really scientific goals, the third and the fourth are only technological applications, and the fifth aim is an educational application of the first four (This, 2006; Yek & Struwe, 2008).

③ Applications of Molecular gastronomy to culinary arts and food

Part food science and part culinary art, molecular gastronomy and its offshoots are revolutionizing food preparation, presentation, and eating and sensory experiences. Contrary to what some might believe to be a fad, this new approach to food has the potential to be nothing short of a revolution in cooking (Yek & Struwe, 2008) (See Figure 4-4).

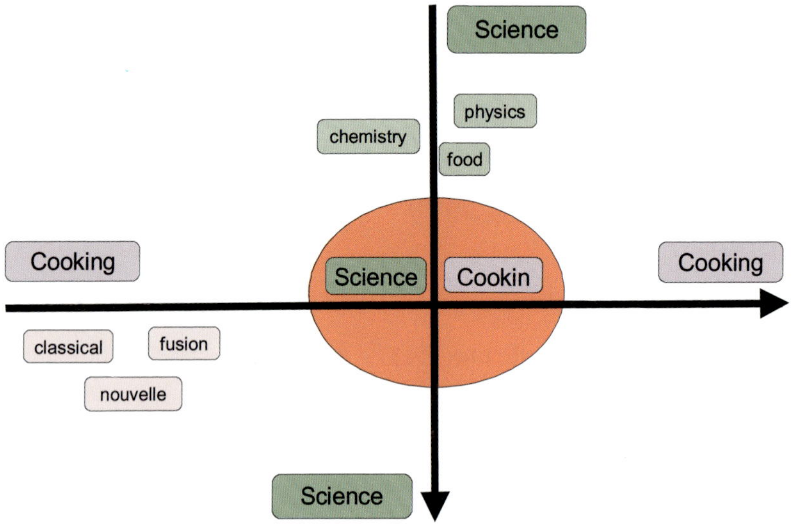

(Source : Yek & Struwe, 2008)

Figure 4-4 Science Meets Cooking

Then what does molecular gastronomy hold for chefs? For them, the scientific exploration of cooking is even more important. Science is the basis for technology and new innovations, so this field will help them to create exciting new dishes and inventions. All sciences are useful for this enterprise, not only chemistry and physics, but also biology, as well as history and sociology. However, for chefs, and hopefully for non-chefs as well, the main aim is to surprise and delight their guests or their family with exciting, tasty and healthy food (This, 2006).

In the most recent ranking of the world's top 50 chefs—by The World's 50 Best Restaurants—the top three chefs were Ferran Adria from El Bulli in Rosas, Spain; Heston Blumenthal from The Fat Duck in Bray, UK; and Pierre Gagnaire from his restaurant in Paris, France for three years of 2006, 2007, and 2008 (Restaurant, 2006, 2007, 2008). In 2009, Adria was first and Blumenthal came second, but

Gagnaire fell to 9th. What is remarkable is that all of these three talented and popular chefs have been inspired by molecular gastronomy.

Since 2005 new dishes have been produced on the basis of the results of molecular gastronomy. It is now the newest fashion for chefs to offer those results to their customers. Here are some examples; fake caviar, burning sherbets, spaghetti made from vegetables, hot ice cream, foam sauces, silky ham powder, crunchy mango purée, and carrot-juice noodles (This, 2005; This, 2006; Duecy, 2008).

Note

- Molecular : relating to or organized from simpler parts
- gastronomy : the art and knowledge involved in preparing and eating good food
- alchemy : a type of chemistry, especially from about the years 1100 to 1500, which dealt with trying to find a way to change ordinary metals into gold and with trying to find a medicine which would cure any disease
- avant-garde : describes creative ideas, styles and methods that are very original or modern in comparison to the period in which they happen; belonging or relating to the avantgarde
- dissertation : a long piece of writing on a particular subject, especially one that is done as a part of a course at college or university
- scrutinize : to examine something very carefully in order to discover information
- offshoot : something which has developed from something larger which already existed
- revolutionize : to completely change something so that it is much better
- fad : a style, activity or interest which is very popular for a short period of time
- nothing short of something : more or less the same as something bad; as bad as something
- hold : to have a particular belief, opinion, or feeling
- exploration : when you search and find out about something

- innovation : (the use of) a new idea or method
- The World's 50 Best Restaurants : The World's 50 Best Restaurants is produced by Restaurant Magazine—a British magazine which produces an annual list of 50 restaurants ranked to be among the best in the world based on a poll of international chefs and critics. The list is published in April of each year (26 April in 2010)

3. Food Miles

① Origin of Food miles

The phrase "food miles" was first coined by UK food policy expert/Professor Tim Lang of London's City University in a report by SAFE Alliance, a British non-profit organization now known as Sustain UK in 1994. Lang describes food miles as the distance that groceries travel to reach consumers' plates (Paxton, 1994; Ballingall & Winchester, 2008).

② Definitions of Food miles

- The macmillandictionary defines food miles as the distance that a food item travels from the place where it is produced to the place where it is eaten (Macmillandictionary, n.d.) (See Figure 4-5).

- Sally Deneen defines a "food mile" as the distance food travels from the farm to the store where you buy it, and these miles are costly to the environment (Deneen, n.d.).

- Tracy Stokes defines food miles as the distance that your food travels from the grower to your plate, including travel to and from processor and retailer (Stokes, 2007).

- Pirog and others define a food mile as the distance food travels from where it is grown or raised to where it is ultimately purchased by the consumer or end-user (Pirog, et al., 2001).

(Source : http://www.ibm.com/smarterplanet/us/en/food_technology/ideas/)

Figure 4-5 In Iowa, the typical carrot traveled 1,600 miles from California

③ Understanding of food miles

The concept of "food miles" presents an argument to buy goods which have travelled the shortest distance from farm to table, and to discriminate against long-haul transportation, especially air-freighted goods. The long-distance transport of food is associated with additional emissions due to increased transportation coupled with greater packaging, as well as a disconnection between the public and local farming. Furthermore, "food miles" encapsulates (and is at the vanguard of) the climate change debate in the UK. In light of growing international concern over the speed and scale of climate change, the concept of "food miles" has captured public attention and apparently is changing some consumers' behaviour, although only around one-third of shoppers know of the concept (MacGregor & Vorley, 2006).

Item	Distance	# of States supplying this item	% Total from Mexico
Grapes	2,143 miles	1	7
Broccoli	2,095 miles	3	3
Asparagus	1,671 miles	5	37
Apples	1,555 miles	8	0
Sweet Corn	813 miles	16	7
Squash	781 miles	12	43
Pumpkins	233 miles	5	0

Each truck represents about 500 miles of distance traveled

* Information for this chart is based on the weighted average source distance, a single distance figure that combines information on distances from production source to consumption or purchase endpoint. For these calculations, USDA Agricultural Marketing Service arrival data for 1998 were used to identify production origin (state or country). Distances from production origin to Chicago were estimated by using a city located in the center of each state as the production origin, and then calculating a one-way road distance to Chicago using the Internet site Mapquest (mapquest.com). Estimations do not include distance from the Chicago Terminal Market to point of retail sale.

Source: Leopold Center for Sustainable Agriculture, http://attra.ncat.org/attra-pub/PDF/foodmiles.pdf

Figure 4-6 Average distance by truck to Chicago Terminal Market (Continental U.S. only)

In America, in a comparison of locally-grown food and long-distance food, researchers at the Leopold Center calculated that local food traveled an average of 44.6 miles to reach its destination compared with 1,546 miles for conventionally-grown and shipped food (See Figure 4-6). The contents of the average European shopping trolley travel 2,200 miles (Blythman, 1993). The calculation may include miles travelled as food is shipped from farms to processors, from processors to storage depots, from storage depots to vendors, and from vendors to consumers. It is a good way of looking at the environmental impact of foods and their ingredients. It includes getting foods to you, but also getting waste foods away from you, and to the landfill. The clear inference is that the further food has to travel, the worse it is for the environment (Ballingall & Winchester, 2008).

In Korea, the local food movement is in the beginning stage. Farmers and consumers organized farmers' market on occasional basis. In some areas, farmers' association has promoted building the local food system and processing locally grown agricultural products. For example, Both Asan Producer Association in which 500 organic agriculture farmers participate and Pureundeul Farming Association which processes and distributes the local food have organized local food system in Cheonan and Asan Province. Pureundeul Farming Association has grown the bean sprouts first, and produced bean curd. Also, In Hoengseong, women peasants formed the association for processing locally grown organic soy. They have been producing and distributing bean curd in the local area (Yoon, n.d.).

④ What individuals can do to reduce food miles

- Learn what foods are in season in your area and try to build your diet around them.

- Shop at a local farmers' market. People living in areas without a farmers' market might try to start one themselves, linking up with interested neighbors and friends and contacting nearby farmers and agricultural officials for help. People can do the same with CSA subscription schemes.

- Eat minimally processed, packaged and marketed food. Generally speaking, the less processing and packaging you see, the less energy went into production and marketing, the less global warming pollution was created.

- Ask the manager or chef of your favorite restaurant how much of the food on the menu is locally grown, and then encourage him or her to source food locally. Urge that the share be increased. People can do the same at their local supermarket or school cafeteria.

- Consolidate trips when grocery shopping. Consider carpooling, public transportation, or a bike trailer for hauling groceries to reduce your personal contribution to food miles.
- Take a trip to a local farm to learn what it produces.
- Limit the amount of meat you consume and when you do buy meat, look for organic or free-range meat produced on sustainable farms.
- Produce a local food directory that lists all the local food sources in your area, including CSA arrangements, farmers' markets, food co-ops, restaurants emphasizing seasonal cuisine and local produce, and farmers willing to sell direct to consumers year-round.
- Buy extra quantities of your favorite fruit or vegetable when it is in season and experiment with drying, canning, jamming, or otherwise preserving it for a later date.
- Plant a garden and grow as much of your own food as possible.
- Speak to your local politician about forming a local food policy council to help guide decisions that affect the local foodshed.

Note

- air-freighted : transport (cargo) by air
- couple : to join or combine

- encapsulate : to express or show the most important facts about something
- the vanguard : a group of people who lead the development of new ideas, or a leading position in the development of something
- the Leopold Center : It was established by the 1987 Iowa Groundwater Protection Act as a research and education center at Iowa State University to develop sustainable agricultural practices that are both profitable and conserve natural resources. The Center is named for Aldo Leopold (1887-1948), a Burlington, Iowa, native known internationally as a conservationist, ecologist, and educator. He saw the need for development of a land ethic, outlined in his 1949 book of essays, A Sand County Almanac.
- landfill : getting rid of large amounts of rubbish by burying it, or a place where rubbish is buried
- inference : when you guess that something is true or form an opinion because of the information that you have
- CSA : CSA stands for Community Supported Agriculture. Consumers support a local farm by "buying a share," which means paying in advance for a specified amount of product. The goods go directly from farmer to buyer as they become available. Pick-up points are generally conveniently located and goods are typically dropped off once a week.
- subscription : an amount of money that you pay regularly to receive a product or service or to be a member of an organization
- scheme : an officially organized plan or system
- urge : to strongly advise or try to persuade someone to do a particular thing
- haul : to pull something heavy slowly and with difficulty
- free-range : relating to or produced by farm animals that are allowed to move around outside and are not kept in cages (= boxes)
- food co-ops(coops) : Food cooperatives are worker or customer owned businesses that provide grocery items of the highest quality and best value to their members. Coops can take the shape of retail stores or buying clubs. All food coops are committed to consumer education, product quality, and member control, and

usually support their local communities by selling produce grown locally by family farms. Use our map to find one near you!

- foodshed : The local food supply system. Local farmers and markets are part of the foodshed.

4. Sustainable Cuisine

① Origin of Sustainable Cuisine

In 1995 Earth Pledge coined the term "Sustainable Cuisine" to describe a derivative of sustainable development that celebrates the pleasures of food and the diversity of cultures, while recognizing the impact of food on our health and our environment. Sustainable Cuisine preserves culinary traditions and addresses the need to safely nourish a growing world population (Earth Pledge, 1995).

② Definition of Sustainable Cuisine

As stated in a 2006 Sustainability Report of Xanterra Parks & Resorts, sustainable cuisine is defined as the practice of using products that are grown, harvested, processed, packaged and distributed with the least amount of environmental impact. Typically these products are local or organic (Sustainability Report of Xanterra, 2006).

③ Sustainable cuisine practices

From chefs' point of view, the heart of sustainable cuisine is very often in their own backyard. Supporting sustainable cuisine means buying from your community farmers' market or greenmarket, and eating the foods that are in season—as much as possible (Conover, 1996).

America's top chefs are leading a culinary charge for sustainable cuisine. Through an organization called the Chefs Collaborative, a growing number of chefs are beginning to examine the origins of the ingredients they purchase and the effect these have had on the environment. The result can be found on the menus of more than 160 restaurants nationwide—food that's good for both the body and the earth (Bogo, 2004). As stated in 2009 Restaurant Industry Pocket Factbook, in the view of customers, 70% of adults said they are more likely to visit a restaurant that offers locally produced food items, and 60% of adults said they are more likely to visit a restaurant that offers food that was grown or raised in an organic or environmentally-friendly way (NRA, 2009).

On the other hand, Earthpledge suggests five tips to practice sustainable cuisine. Let's look at them (Earth Pledge, n.d.);

- Purchasing sustainably and locally grown/raised products
- Using ingredients that are seasonal and plentiful (not in danger of depletion)
- Purchasing product locally, and encouraging local purveyors to provide diverse products including heirloom varieties and rare breeds

- Minimizing waste by using all edible parts of a product (i.e. making stock out of scraps and bones), composting, and recycling

④ Managing Food Costs When Running a Sustainable Kitchen

The first goal of any restaurant is to sustain their business. Managing food costs is central to running a strong business, but can be a challenge when you"re committed to buying local, seasonal, and sustainably produced food. The Chefs Collaborative member chefs we spoke with about their food purchasing habits keep local, seasonal, and sustainable food central in their purchasing frameworks and routinely keep food costs under 32% of expenses. It's a good idea to develop your own framework for making purchasing decisions and let vendors know your criteria. Let's look at five successful strategies and approaches our members have taken (Chefs Collaborative, 2009).

- Strive for 100% utilization
- Look at the menu as a whole rather than at any individual item
- Start with what's easiest
- Start with what's local and in season and move out
- Using the whole animal can make money. (as well as using underutilized cuts of meat)

Note

- Chefs Collaborative : This is the leading nonprofit network of chefs that fosters a sustainable food system through advocacy, education, and collaboration with the broader food community.
- Earth Pledge : It is a nonprofit organization devoted to identifying and promoting innovative techniques and technologies that restore the balance between human

and natural systems. Through demonstrations, education and research, the nonprofit organization delivers viable modes to government, industry and community for implementing replicable solutions that will inspire and help facilitate a global transition to sustainability. Its Green Roofs Initiative supports the development of green, vegetated rooftops in urban areas to prevent storm water run-off and pollution; lower temperatures in cities; and improve air quality.

- derivative : a form of something, such as a word, made or developed from another form
- address : to give attention to or deal with a matter or problem
- nourish : to provide people or living things with food in order to make them grow and keep them healthy
- charge : the responsibility or duty of looking after somebody or something
- deplete : to reduce something in size or amount, especially supplies of energy, money, etc.
- purveyor : a business which provides goods or services
- heirloom : a valuable object that has been given by older members of a family to younger members of the same family over many years
- breed : particular type of animal or plant
- scraps : small bits of food which have not been eaten and which are usually thrown away
- strive : to try very hard to do something or to make something happen, especially for a long time or against difficulties
- compost : to convert organic matter to compost, or to be converted to compost
- move out : to stop living in a particular home
- underutilize : to fail to utilize fully:

5. Food Deserts

① Origin of Food deserts

The term 'desert' was first used to describe an urban environment lacking in certain facilities as far back as 1973 when J. BAINES (The Environment) wrote "The large suburban estates that are a recent feature of the townscape are epitomized by the regular rows of similarly styled houses that have earned for themselves the title of suburban deserts. They often lack the shops, churches, public houses, and social centers that allow a community life to develop"(Shaw, 2008).

② Definitions of Food deserts

- In 1996, Low Income Project Team of the Nutrition Task Force defines food deserts as areas of relative exclusion where people experience physical and economic barriers to accessing healthy food (Hobbiss, 2000).

- In 1997, the Independent defines food deserts as those areas of inner cities where cheap nutritious food is virtually unobtainable. Car-less residents, unable to reach out-of-town supermarkets, depend on the corner shop where prices are high, products are processed and fresh fruit and vegetables are poor or non-existent (Laurence, 1997).

- In 1997, Tessa Jowell, UK Government Health Minister, defines food deserts as an area where people do not have easy access to healthy, fresh foods, particularly if they are poor and have limited mobility (Furey et al., 1999).

③ Understanding of food deserts

In the United States, food deserts tend to be located in urban and rural low-income neighborhoods, where residents are less likely to have access to supermarkets or grocery stores that provide healthy food choices. For communities with few food retailers or supermarkets that stock little or no fresh produce, low-fat dairy, whole grains, and other healthy foods, those populations may be more likely to suffer from high rates of diabetes, cardiovascular disease, and obesity (Whitacre et al., 2009).

In the view of Wikipedia the concept of 'access' may be interpreted in three ways. Let's look at them (Wikipedia, n.d.).

- 'Physical access' to shops can be difficult if the shops are distant, the shopper is elderly or infirm, the area has many hills, public transport links are poor, and the consumer has no car. Also, the shop may be across a busy road, difficult to cross with children or with underpasses that some fear to use because of a crime risk. For some, such as the disabled, the inside of the shop may be hard to access physically if there are steps up or the interior is cramped with no room for walking aids. Carrying fresh food home may also be hard for some.

- 'Financial access' is difficult if the consumer lacks the money to buy healthy foods (generally more expensive, calorie for calorie, than less healthy, sugary, and fatty 'junk foods') or if the shopper cannot afford the bus fare to remote shops selling fresh foods and instead uses local fast food outlets. Other forms of financial access barriers may be inability to afford storage space for food, or for the very poor, living in temporary accommodation that does not offer good cooking facilities.

- Mental attitude or food knowledge of the consumer may prevent them accessing fresh vegetables. They may lack cooking knowledge or have the idea that eating a healthy diet isn't important.

Note

- suburban : relating to, belonging to, or located in a suburb
- estate : a group of houses or factories built in a planned way
- exclusion : when someone or something is not allowed to take part in an activity or to enter a place
- diabetes : a disease in which the body cannot control the level of sugar in the blood
- cardiovascular : relating to the heart and blood vessels (= tubes that carry blood around the body)

- obesity : more than average fatness
- infirm : ill or needing care, especially for long periods and often because of old age
- underpass : a road or path that goes under something such as a busy road, allowing vehicles or people to go from one side to the other
- cramp : to limit someone, especially to prevent them from enjoying a full life
- calorie for calorie : ex) It also compared foods on a like-for-like (calorie-for-calorie) basis, to understand their relative effect on energy intake.
- like-for-like (not comparable) : Pertaining to an action which replaces one thing with another of the same type. ex) The soccer coach made a like-for-like substitution, replacing the injured defender with another defensive player.
- accommodation : a place to live, work, stay, etc. in

6. Culinary Tourism

① Origin of Culinary Tourism

The term "Culinary Tourism" is a relatively new one, first coined in 1998 by Lucy Long, an Assistant Professor of Popular Culture at Bowling Green State University (Ely, 2007). In fact, culinary tourism as an industry did not coming into being until the year 2001, when International Culinary Tourism Association (ICTA) President Erik Wolf distributed his culinary tourism white paper (ICTA, 2003).

② Definitions of Culinary Tourism

As stated by ICTA, in its broadest sense, culinary tourism is defined as the pursuit of unique and memorable culinary experiences of all kinds, often while traveling, but one can also be a culinary tourist at home (ICTA, 2003). Wolf defines it as the pursuit of prepared food/drink as an attraction-both for visitors and locals alike (Wolf, 2008).

③ Scope of Culinary Tourism

Food can be an attraction in tourism. Food and wine can be the impetus behind a visit to another city or country. Unlike other travel activities and attractions, cuisine is available year-round, any time of day and in any weather. A unique food and drink experience has the power to lure tourists like museums, recreation and shopping. Because regional foods and recipes are a major part of what makes one place different from another, restaurants should create unique and memorable food and drink experiences to build excitement and develop a competitive advantage. Your restaurant may already be contributing to culinary tourism in your community without even knowing it (Quantified Marketing Group, 2010).

Culinary tourism includes any unique or memorable dining experience that a traveler encounters. Because dining is one of the best ways visitors can get to know a new and exotic locale, culinary tourism is the hottest niche to emerge within the travel industry in years (Quantified Marketing Group, 2010). Research indicates that Culinary Tourism is a lucrative niche market that holds strong potential for economic and community development (MDAR, 2010).

In Korea many efforts and movements are being made and developed towards the globalization of Korean cuisine. We can come up with culinary tourism to promote it to the world.

Culinary tourism serves as an avenue through which the globalization of Korean cuisine can be promoted. The culinary tourist comes to taste the cuisine, learn how to make it and visit a brewery, tea plantation or farm or two (Oh, Jean, 2009).

Culinary Tourism is not just experiences of the highest caliber—that would be gourmet tourism. This is perhaps best illustrated by the notion that Culinary Tourism is about what is "unique and memorable, not what is necessarily pretentious and exclusive (wikipedia, 2010)." Therefore the phrase "unique and memorable" is key to understanding culinary tourism.

Culinary Tourism is not agritourism. While the seeds of cuisine are in agriculture, and agriculture and cuisine are inextricably linked, the two are very different. Agritourism is a subset of rural tourism, while cuisine is a subset of cultural tourism, as cuisine is a manifestation of culture (ICTA, 2003).

Here is a subset of cultural tourism. Higher-end experiences fall into a subset of culinary tourism called "Gourmet Tourism". Similarly, wine tourism, beer tourism and spa tourism are also regarded as subsets of culinary tourism (ICTA, 2003).

③ Culinary Tourism Activities

Deliberate culinary travelers are more likely than others to participate in a variety of other food-and-wine-related activities. These activities are as follows (Wolf, 2008; TTIA, 2009);

- See the chef/owner of a noted restaurant make a guest appearance, or even a nightly performance
- See chefs compete
- Eat/drink at, or attend the grand opening of, or special event at, a new or famous restaurant or bar
- Eat/drink at a hard-to-find "locals-only" restaurant or bar
- Participate in a food, wine or beer special event/festival
- Search for unique ingredients (e.g. at a grocery, roadside stand or farmers' market, bazaar, or "u-pick" herbs, fruits and vegetables on local farms)
- Drive a wine route
- Attend cooking classes (e.g. for a few days, weeks or months)
- Visit with a chef/owner of a local restaurant
- Pick-your-own fruits, vegetables and herbs
- Shopping for local cookbooks/kitchen gadget
- Visit a local pastry shop, an interesting bar on a nameless street that only locals know about, the pretzel vendor on the streets of New York City, or a gelato vendor on a historic street in Italy
- Watch chef demonstrations or in-the-kitchen chef training
- Have a memorable experience sitting at the chef's table located directly in front of the kitchen

④ Culinary Tourism Today

Judging by the surge since 2001 in the number of times "culinary tourism" has appeared as a subject matter or in a session title in tourism industry conferences and programs, we can see that Culinary Tourism is valued by tourism industry professionals as one of the most popular niches in the world's tourism industry. This makes sense, given recent consumer focus on healthy and organic eating, culinary/food pedigrees, and the simple fact that all travelers must eat. Not every visitor goes shopping or visits museums, but all travelers eat. For anyone who doubts, look at the increase in cooking shows featured on The Travel Channel [Anthony Bourdain No Reservations] or travel shows featured on The Food Network [Rachel Ray's $40 a Day series], as examples (Wikipedia, 2009).

Since its true birth as an industry in 2003, culinary tourism has grown exponentially every year, as measured by a number of indicators. First the number of consumers interested in the subject matter has grown which is documented by the increase in culinary travel shows on television. One sees food shows on travel channels and travel shows on food channels. There continues to be a strong crossover of these industries (ICTA, 2003).

⑤ Culinary Travelers' Propensity

Texas Travel Industry Association shows Culinary Travelers' Propensity in USA as follows (TTIA, 2009);

- On average culinary travelers spend over one-third (36%) of their personal travel budget on food-related activities
- In terms of food travel destinations, California (14%) and Florida (10%) are most common, followed by New York (7%) and Texas (6%)

- Among those interested in future culinary activities, going to restaurants for unique and memorable experiences and local/regional cuisine top the list. Large shares also report they are interested in visiting farmers markets (83%), sampling traditional artisan products (81%), attending culinary festivals (77%), tasting locally made wines (72%) or touring wineries (71%)
- Serious culinary travelers are more likely to:

  *Be upscale in terms of their education and income

  *Participate in a wide variety of other trip activities ranging from shopping and spa services to cultural and heritage-related activities to outdoor/nature-based experiences

  *Choose a destination to experience local culture and cuisine

  *Spend more money per trip, especially for food and wine

  *Be active information seekers, relying heavily on word-of-mouth and a variety of print publications, as well as using online information resources

⑥ Facts of Culinary Tourism

Culinary Tourism Society BC promoting the potential for culinary tourism in British Columbia, Canada shows some facts of culinary tourism as follows (CTSBC, 2010);

- Cuisine is a saleable experience.
- Dining is the most memorable tourism experience.
- Nearly 100% of tourists dine out when traveling.
- Dining is consistently one of the top three favourite tourist activities.
- The higher the dinner bill, the more likely the patrons are tourists.
- Many culinary tourists are affluent individuals earning above average incomes.

- Interest in cuisine in travel is not reserved to a particular age, sex, or ethnic group.
- Unlike other travel activities and attractions, cuisine is available year-round, any time of day and in any weather.
- Cuisine is "experiential" as it satisfies new traveler demands for hands-on, interactive experiences.
- Dining is a way to experience local culture.
- Directing tourists to exemplary cuisine experiences adds value to tourist's trips resulting in increased tourism spending, longer stays and repeat visits.

⑦ Getting Started in Culinary Tourism

To get started in culinary tourism, Texas Travel Industry Association recommends that we first inventory our local product as follows (TTIA, 2009);

- Restaurants and bakeries (Specifically those featuring local or regional fare)
- Wineries/microbreweries
- Gourmet food producers
- Orchards/farms
- Bed and Breakfasts offering gourmet breakfasts
- Coffee houses
- Kitchen shops
- Local or regional cookbooks
- Cooking or culinary schools
- Culinary festivals and events

Note

- assistant professor : a member of a college or university faculty ranking typically above an instructor and below an associate professor
- come into being : be born or come into existence
- impetus : something which encourages a particular activity or makes that activity more energetic or effective
- niche : an area or position which is exactly suitable for a small group of the same type
- come up with : to think of, develop, or find something
- avenue : a method or way of doing something; a possibility
- pretentious : trying to appear or sound more important or clever than you are, especially in matters of art and literature
- exclusive : ① expensive and only for people who are rich or of a high social class, ② limited to only one person or group of people
- agriculture : farming
- subset : a set (= group of similar numbers, objects or people) that is part of another, larger set
- manifestation : a sign of something existing or happening
- high-end : expensive and likely to appeal to sophisticated and discerning people
- fall into : be included in or classified as
- Deliberate : describes a movement, action or thought which is done carefully without hurrying
- make a guest appearance : 찬조출연하다
- gadget : a small device or machine with a particular purpose
- pretzel : a crisp salted knot-shaped or stick-shaped biscuit with a golden brown glaze
- gelato : an Italian ice cream made from milk, gelatin, sugar, and fruit
- pedigree : a person's family history, education and experience, or the history of an idea or activity
- crossover : the process or result of changing from one activity or style to another

- propensity : a tendency towards a particular way of behaving, especially a bad one
- upscale(US for upmarket) : intended or designed for wealthy consumers
- word-of-mouth : communication using the spoken word
- winery : a place where wine is made
- microbrewery : a small company which makes beer, usually using traditional methods, and which often has a restaurant where its beer is served
- gourmet : ① (of food) very high quality, ex) gourmet coffee, a gourmet meal ② producing or serving food which is very high quality ex) a gourmet restaurant, a gourmet chef
- orchard : an area of land where fruit trees (but not orange trees or other citrus trees) are grown
- Bed and Breakfast(abbreviation B & B, also B and B) : a room to sleep in for the night and a morning meal, or a private house or small hotel offering this

7. Culinology®

① Origin of Culinology®

Culinology (culinary arts + food technology) is a word coined by Winston Riley, the first president and founder of the Research Chefs Association. "Culinology" is a registered trademark with a first use from 1999. Culinology is also the name of the official magazine (since 2003) of the Research Chefs Association. Culinologists seek to make food taste better, be safer to eat, be easier to grow and distribute, etc. The term "food science" might be more used than "culinology" because of the latter term's existing trademark (Popik, 2009).

② Understanding of Culinology

Culinology® is the blending of the disciplines of food science and culinary arts. By combining the knowledge of basic science with the creativity of culinary arts, students develop a unique skill set that will enable them to define the future of food through the creative process of developing new food products (Clemson, n.d.).

The Research Chef is first a chef, a culinarian, a food focused individual, dedicated to producing the finest possible combination of ingredients to achieve palate pleasing results whether personally preparing the product for the customer they know or one they will never know. The Research Chef is also a researcher who uses scientific methods and knowledge to insure their creativity can be enjoyed far beyond the confines of their kitchen or laboratory. A true Chef is an artist and a gourmet, a manager and a leader. A true Food Scientist is a technologist and statistician, an engineer and a nutritionist. A Culinologist is a skilled chef who is creating a new generation of exciting, high quality convenience food products (SMSUb, n.d.).

Tom Pearson, Ph.D., professor and director of graduate programs in the restaurant, hotel, institutional and tourism management department of Purdue University, West Lafayette, IN, undertook a study to come up with a set of descriptors for a research chef/culinologist. But his results were two. One describes a more research-directed culinologist, primarily involved in the commercial development of new products and processes. This type possesses strong food-ingredient knowledge and culinary expertise. The second type of culinologist is more management-focused, and is involved in strategic planning, working with customers and doing presentations.

Pearson's study also found that RCA members exhibited 46 "knowledge competencies," 38 "skill and ability competencies" and 23 "behavior competencies." The most statistically significant competencies, in order of mean response, were (Cousminer, 1999):

- A sense of taste
- A "passion" about food
- Ability to work with customers
- Knowledge of flavors
- Knowledge of recipe development
- Ability to work as part of a product development team
- Knowledge of food sanitation
- Ability to distinguish levels of quality in food products

- General communication skills
- Self-confidence and a positive attitude
- Being enthusiastic
- Ability to make decisions
- Action oriented/willing to accept responsibility(organized, intellectually, curious, and proactive)
- Knowledge of culinary fundamentals/production systems
- Creativity
- Knowledge of functional ingredients
- Dedication to one's profession
- Ability to see the "big picture"
- Understanding of complete product development process—benchtop through commercial production
- Management skills: personnel development, ability to prioritize, ability to delegate
- Knowledge of food trends
- Knowledge of foodservice operations
- Knowledge of food trends—past/present/future
- Knowledge of ethnic/regional cuisines—preparation/spicing/presentation
- Skilled in basic computer systems

Knowing these competencies, how then are we developing our certifications/ qualifications? By considering the following factors:

- Culinary education or training at establishments such as the Culinary Institute of America, Hyde Park, NY; Johnson and Wales University, Providence, RI; and Nicholls State University, Thibodaux, LA

- Culinary and foodservice experience gained from working "in the trenches"—i.e., hotel and restaurant kitchens
- Scientific and technical education in the food science, food management, food processing and food marketing areas, obtained from both formal instruction and "on the job" training
- Scientific and technical expertise gained by working for food manufacturers, ingredient suppliers or multi-unit chain operators
- Membership in the RCA

③ Educational programs for future culinologists

Universities and colleges around the country are offering degrees in culinology. The training blends the science and technology associated with food production and preservation research with the cooking or culinary artistry of chefs who strive to create the quality taste, texture and visual appeal that consumers look for in food. Schools are now coming to the RCA for advice on starting culinology programs. Here are some select course offerings(Cornwell, 2005; RCA, unknown era).

- Clemson University offers Culinary Science (Culinology®) program, as one of 7 Emphasis Areas, within The Food Science and Human Nutrition department. At Clemson, Culinology® is integrated into our Food Science Degree program as an emphasis area. Students choosing this emphasis area take additional culinary focused courses along with their traditional food science courses like food chemistry that have Culinology® integrated into their teaching (i.e. the science and art of food emulsions). Students interested in new product development and entrepreneurship typically choose this emphasis area.
  Approved by the Research Chefs Association and the Institute of Food Technologist Clemson is the only university in the country with a program

approved by both professional organizations(clemson, unknown era; RCA, unknown era).

- Orange Coast Community College offers a certificate program in Culinology® and courses at OCC include Culinary Arts and Food Science and prepare you to transfer to California State University, Pomona in Food Science and Technology with a emphasis in Culinology(OCC, unknown era; RCA, unknown era).

- California State University, Pomona offers Bachelor of Science in Food Science and Technology, with a Track in Culinology®. Students take two years of culinary classes at Orange Coast Community College and finish with two years of Food Science and Technology, with a Track in Culinology® at the university(csupomona, unknown era; RCA, unknown era).

- The University of Massachusetts-Amherst offers a unique program in Culinology®, within The Department of Food Science, that has been accredited by the Research Chefs Association. This program combines culinary arts and food science by accepting students with a two-year culinary arts degree and providing them with a science-oriented framework that enables them to obtain a B.S. in Food Science from the University of Massachusetts Amherst in three years(umass, unknown era; RCA, unknown era).

- Dominican University offers a culinology degree program. Students typically transfer into Dominican University with a two-year associate's degree from an accredited culinary arts program and add the additional years of food science and general liberal arts requirements to obtain the bachelor's degree in Nutrition and Dietetics. However, students can begin their career with a food science major and integrate the culinary degree either within that degree or after the basic food science degree is awarded(dom, unknown era; RCA, unknown era).

- The University of Cincinnati's Applied Science and Cincinnati State Technical and Community College offer a new baccalaureate degree in Culinary Arts and Science. This unique dual enrollment program has students spending their first two years at Cincinnati State and then completing their bachelor's degree at UC. This is the first culinary program of its kind in Ohio and only the third in the U.S(UC, unknown era; RCA, unknown era).

- Southwest Minnesota State University(SMSU)'s Bachelor of Science in Culinology® is the only degree of its kind in the world. SMSU holds the distinction of being the only Research Chefs Association's approved Culinology® program that is an independent, stand-alone, fully integrated culinary arts and food science program(SMSUb, unknown era). Students majoring in Culinology® can also obtain a Minor in Business Administration or a Minor in Marketing during the Junior and Senior year(SMSUb, unknown era).

④ Employment Outlook for Culinologists

Culinologists are in high demand all across the country. Graduates with a Bachelor's degree relating to Culinology® program will be employed with a starting salary of $52,000. Let me show an example of SMSU to you.

A wide variety of job opportunities are available to SMSU graduates. Graduates may go to work with major food manufacturers, custom manufacturing facilities, restaurant chains, etc., in positions such as: Research and Development Chef, TecnoChef™, Product Development Manager, Corporate Chef, Culinary Research and Development Director, Culinary Research Technologist, Savory Lab Manager, Product Formulation Chef, and Manager of Culinology. Culinologists receive holidays and weekends off and make anywhere from $45,000 to $100,000. The starting salary for a SMSU Culinology® graduate is $52,000 in 2008(SMSUa, unknown era).

Note

- RCA : The RCA has been created by folks who consider themselves culinologists, either by training or by job description. The association is dedicated to the care and feeding, growth, development and promotion of culinology and those who practice its unique blend of art and science.
- trademark : a name or a symbol which is put on a product to show that it is made by a particular producer and which cannot be legally used by any other producer
- confines : the outer limits of something
- descriptor : a word or phrase used to categorize records in a database so that all records containing the key can be retrieved together
- competency : an important skill that is needed to do a job
- sanitation : the systems for taking dirty water and other waste products away from buildings in order to protect people's health
- proactive : taking action by causing change and not only reacting to change when it happens
- big picture : the entire perspective on a situation or issue—used with the
- benchtop : suitable (as in size or configuration) for convenient use on a laboratory workbench <a benchtop centrifuge>
- prioritize : to decide which of a group of things are the most important so that you can deal with them first
- delegate : to give a particular job, duty, right, etc. to someone else so that they do it for you

- trench : a place, position, or level at which an activity is carried on in a manner likened to trench warfare—often used in the phrase in the trenches <activists working in the trenches>
- expertise : a high level of knowledge or skill
- multi-unit : 다점포
- artistry : great skill in creating or performing something, such as in writing, music, sport, etc.
- emulsion : a mixture that results when one liquid is added to another and is mixed with it but does not dissolve into it
- accredit : to officially recognize, accept or approve of someone or something
- baccalaureate : a bachelor's degree (formal)
- stand-alone : Something, such as a computer or a business, which is stand-alone can operate on its own without needing help from another similar thing.
- minor : secondary to the major course of study
- outlook : the likely future situation

References

Blythman, Joanna, 1993, "Eat local and sever the food chains," The Independent, October 23

Halweil, Brian, 2002, "Home Grown: The Case for Local Food in a Global Market," Washington, DC: Worldwatch, November 2002.

Hobbiss, Reisig V., 2000, "Food deserts and how to tackle item: A study of one city's approach," Health Education Journal, 59:137-149.

Laurence, J., 1997, "The Independent newspaper." London, UK, 11 Jun.

Paxton, A. 1994, "The Food Miles Report: The dangers of long distance food transport," London: Safe Alliance.

This, H., 2005, "Molecular gastronomy," Nature Materials, 4(1), 5-7

Yek, Grace S., Kurt Struwe, 2008, "Deconstructing Molecular Gastronomy," Food Technology, 62(6):34-45

Ballingall, John and Niven Winchester, 2008, "Food miles: Starving the poor?," University of Otago Economics Discussion Papers No. 0812, Dec., Retrieved Jan. 13, 2010 from http://www.commerce.otago.ac.nz/ECON/research /discussionpapers/DP_0812.pdf

Bogo, Jennifer, 2004, "Audubon at Home Web Exclusive: When Conservation Meets Cuisine," Audubon, 5/2004, Retrieved Jan. 13, 2010 from http://audubonmagazine.org/features0405/chefs_web.html

Chefs Collaborative, 2009, "Five Tips for Managing Food Costs When Running a Sustainable Kitchen," Retrieved Jan. 13, 2010 from http://chefscollaborative.org/wp-content/uploads/2009/11/Five-Tips-for-Managing-Food-Costs-When-Running-a-Sustainable-Restaurant-Kitchen-FINAL.pdf

Clemson, "Culinology Emphasis Area," Retrieved Jan. 5, 2010 from http://www.clemson.edu/cafls/departments/foodscience/undergraduate/culinology.html

Conover, Kirsten A., 1996, "Eat your vegetables!' takes on fresh meaning," April 17, Retrieved Jan. 13, 2010 from http://www.lasvegassun.com/news/1996/apr/17/eat-your-vegetables-takes-on-fresh-meaning/

Cornwell, Lisa, 2005, "New degree programs produce chef-scientists," Aug. 14, Retrieved Jan. 5, 2010 from http://www.usatoday.com/tech/news/techinnovations/2005-08-14-culinology_x.htm

Cousminer, Jeffrey, 1999, "Practicing Culinology," Jan. 1, Retrieved Jan. 5, 2010 from http://www.foodproductdesign.com/articles/1999/01/practicing-culinology.aspx

Csupomona, "Food science & Technology: Culinology®," Retrieved Jan. 6, 2010 from http://www.csupomona.edu/~agri/academics/foodtechnology.shtml#bachelor

Davey, Robert, 2004, "Dear Earth Talk: What on Earth is this "Slow Food" movement I keep hearing about?," May, Retrieved Dec. 20, 2009 from http://www.foodreference.com/html/a-slow-food.html

Deneen, Sally, "food miles," Retrieved Jan. 13, 2010 from http://www.thedailygreen.com/living-green/definitions/Food-Miles

Dom, "Culinology: Majors," Retrieved Jan. 6, 2010 from http://www.dom.edu/ican/academics/information/culinology.html

Duecy, Erica, 2008, "La Nueva Cocina: Spain's New Cuisine," Retrieved Jan. 3, 2010 from http://www.fodors.com/news/story_2310.html

Ely, Susan, 2007, "HUNGRY FOR ADVENTURE; Culinary tourism, travel decisions based on food, Food and Travel," 28-33, Retrieved Jan. 10, 2010 from http://www.saintjacquesfrenchcuisine.com/Hungry.pdf

Furey, Sinead, Heather McIlveen, and Christopher Strugnell, 1999, "Food Deserts: An Issue of Social Justice," Oct. 1999, 2(6), Retrieved Jan. 11, 2010 from http://journal.media-culture.org.au/9910/deserts.php

Hill, Holly, 2008, "Food Miles: Background and Marketing," NCAT, Retrieved Jan. 13, 2010 from http://attra.ncat.org/attra-pub/PDF/foodmiles.pdf

ICTA, 2003, "Introduction to culinary tourism," Retrieved Jan. 11, 2010 from http://www.culinarytourism.org/?page=intro

MacGregor, James; Bill Vorley, 2006, "Sustainable development opinion," IIED, Retrieved Jan. 13, 2010 from http://www.iied.org/pubs/pdfs/11064IIED.pdf

Maharaj, Joshna, 2009, "Memo to the Chef: Embracing Slow Food," Retrieved Jan. 13, 2010 from http://fsn.dgtlpub.com/2009/2009-10-31/home.php?page_view=22

Matsey, Jonathan, 2003, "You are what you eat," Retrieved Dec. 20, 2009 from http://www.nyc24.org/2003/issue1/story3/page2.html

MDAR, 2010, "Culinary Tourism Initiative," Massachusetts Department of Agricultural Resources, Retrieved Jan. 10, 2010 from http://www.mass.gov/agr/markets/culinary_tourism.htm

NRA, 2009, "Restaurant Industry Pocket Factbook," Retrieved Jan. 10, 2010 from http://www.restaurant.org/pdfs/research/2009Factbook.pdf

OCC, "Interested in a career in Food Science/Culinology, this is the place," Retrieved Jan. 6, 2010 from http://www.orangecoastcollege.edu/academics/divisions/consumer_health/food_science/

Oh, Jean, 2009, "[SAVOR KOREA (7)] Korean food could be next big thing," The Korea Herald, Nov. 26. Retrieved Jan. 11, 2010 from http://www.koreaherald.co.kr/NEWKHSITE/data/html_dir/2009/11/26/200911260051.asp

Pirog, Rich; Van Pelt, Timothy; Enshayan, Kamyar; Cook, Ellen, 2001, "Food, Fuel, and Freeways: An Iowa perspective on how far food travels, fuel usage, and greenhouse gas emissions," Leopold Center for Sustainable Agriculture, Iowa State University, June, Retrieved Jan. 13, 2010 from http://www.leopold.iastate.edu/pubs/staff/ppp/food_mil.pdf

Popik, Barry, 2009, "Culinology (culinary + technology)," Entry from October 26, Retrieved Jan. 5, 2010 from http://www.barrypopik.com/index.php /new_york_city/entry/culinology_culinary_technology/

RCA, "RCA-Approved Culinology® Programs," Retrieved Jan. 5, 2010 from http://www.culinology.com/rca-approved-programs

Restaurant, 2006, The World's 50 Best Restaurants, Retrieved Jan. 3, 2010 from www.theworlds50best.com

Restaurant, 2007, The World's 50 Best Restaurants, Retrieved Jan. 3, 2010 from www.theworlds50best.com

Restaurant, 2008, The World's 50 Best Restaurants, Retrieved Jan. 3, 2010 from www.theworlds50best.com

Restaurant, 2009, The World's 50 Best Restaurants, Retrieved Jan. 3, 2010 from . www.theworlds50best.com

Quantified Marketing Group, 2010, "Food is the attraction," Retrieved Jan. 11, 2010 from http://www.quantifiedmarketing.com/learning_center/food-attraction.php

Shaw, Hillary, 2008, "What is a 'food desert'?", Jun. Retrieved Jan. 11, 2010 from http://www.fooddeserts.org/images/whatisfd.htm

SMSUa, "ACADEMIC PROGRAMS: Culinology®," Retrieved Jan. 11, 2010 from http://www.smsu.edu/Catalog/catalog_pdf/culinology.pdf

SMSUb, Culinology, Retrieved Jan. 5, 2010 from http://www.smsu.edu/Academics /Programs/Culinology/Index.cfm

Stokes, Tracy, 2007, "10 ways to reduce food miles," May, Retrieved Jan. 13, 2010 from http://www.ecostreet.com/blog/sustainable-lifestyle/2007/05/22 /10-ways-to-reduce-food-miles/

This, H., 2006, "Food for tomorrow? How the scientific discipline of molecular gastronomy could change the way we eat," Retrieved Jan. 3, 2010 from http://www.nature.com/embor/journal/v7/n11/full/7400850.html

TIA and Edge Research, 2006, "Profile of Culinary Travelers," Sponsored by Gourmet,

Edge Research and International and Oregon Culinary Tourism Association

TTIA, 2009, "A Taste of Culinary Tourism," Retrieved Jan. 11, 2010 from http://www.ttia.org/resource/resmgr/Workshops09/Culinary_Tourism.pdf

UC, "Culinary Arts and Science Program," Retrieved Jan. 6, 2010 from http://www.uc.edu/cas/cht/culinary/

Umass, "Food Science: Culinary Science." Retrieved Jan. 6, 2010 from http://www.umass.edu/ug_programguide/foodsci.html

Whitacre, Paula, Tarnapol Peggy Tsai, and Janet Mulligan, 2009, "The Public Health Effects of Food Deserts: Workshop Summary," National Research Council, Retrieved Jan. 11, 2010 from http://www.nap.edu/openbook.php?record_id=12623&page=5

Wolf, Erik, 2008, "Culinary Tourism-A Hot and Fresh Idea," Tourism Review, Dec. 4-6, Retrieved Jan. 10, 2010 from www.tourism-review.com/

Yoon, Byeong-Seon, unknown era, "Keeping the food sovereignty through the local food movement," Konkuk University, Retrieved Jan. 13, 2010 from http://www.irsa-world.org/XII/papers/3-10.pdf

Retrieved Jan. 13, 2010 from http://www.prairielandcsa.org/whatisacsa.html

Retrieved Jan. 13, 2010 from http://www.localharvest.org/food-coops/

Retrieved Jan. 13, 2010 from http://dictionary.cambridge.org/

Retrieved Jan. 13, 2010 from http://www.macmillandictionary.com/

Retrieved Jan. 6, 2010 from http://idioms.thefreedictionary.com/

Retrieved Jan. 6, 2010 from http://encarta.msn.com/encnet/features/dictionary/

Retrieved Jan. 5, 2010 from http://www.merriam-webster.com/dictionary/

Retrieved Jan. 11, 2010 from http://en.wikipedia.org/wiki/Food_desert

Retrieved Jan. 11, 2010 from http://idioms.thefreedictionary.com/

Retrieved Jan. 11, 2010 from http://en.wiktionary.org/wiki/like-for-like

Retrieved Jan. 13, 2010 from http://www.earthpledge.org/

Retrieved Jan. 13, 2010 from http://www.xanterra.com/sustainable-cuisine-385.html

Retrieved Jan. 13, 2010 from http://www.cleanaircommunities.org/newsroom/pr050929silvercup.pdf

Retrieved Jan. 3, 2010 from http://www.slowfoodbeirut.org/convivium/defconv.html

Retrieved Jan. 3, 2010 from http://www.slowfoodfoundation.com/eng/

Retrieved Jan. 3, 2010 from http://www.slowfoodfoundation.org/eng/

Retrieved Jan. 3, 2010 from http://www.terramadre.org/pagine/welcome.lasso?n=en

Retrieved Jan. 3, 2010 from http://www.slowfood.com/

Retrieved Jan. 3, 2010 from http://en.wikipedia.org/wiki/Restaurant_(magazine)_Top_50

Retrieved Jan. 13, 2010 from http://www.ibm.com/smarterplanet/us/en/food_technology/ideas/

Chapter 05

Using Herbs and Spices

Knowledge and understanding
about herbs and spices is imperative.

This information is provided by University of Delaware Cooperative Extension. For young students much knowledge about herbs and spices grows ever imperative. Having a basic knowledge in herbs and spices is to raise your competitiveness in the culinary industry. Let's learn more about herbs and spices.

Although spices and herbs have been used since ancient times, they are playing a new and important role in modern food preparation. They not only add unique flavors to our food, but contribute color and variety as well. Certain spices and herbs used alone, or in blends, can replace or reduce salt and sugar in foods (Snider, 2007).

1. What are Spices and Herbs?

Many people use the terms interchangeably to mean any product of plant origin used primarily for seasoning food. Technically, herbs come from aromatic plants grown in the temperate zone, while spices are products of tropical plants. Usually, the leaves of herbs are used; whereas, spices may come from the bark, berries, flower buds, roots, or seeds.

2. Do Herbs and Spices add Any Nutritive Value to Foods?

Herbs and spices add very little if any nutritive value to foods—they are used only for flavoring or coloring foods. In general, they are low in calories, sodium, fat and cholesterol, although some of the oil-rich seeds, such as poppy and sesame, contain a moderate amount of calories. Also, some seasonings, such as celery or parsley flakes, contain enough sodium to be counted. However, these ingredients are used in such small quantities that they are not a problem unless a recipe calls for an unusually large amount, or unless the diet restriction is severe.

3. Using Herbs and Spices

The advice frequently offered today is simply, "In place of salt, use herbs and spices for flavor." This leaves one wondering: Which spice with what food? How much? In what combination? Here are some starting points:

- Because herbs and spices are expensive, start with some of the basic herbs and spices. Americans particularly like pepper, basil, oregano and cinnamon.
- To become familiar with the flavor of a specific herb, mix it with butter, margarine, or cream cheese, let it stand for at least an hour, then taste this mixture on a cracker.
- Each spice or herb has a distinctive flavor, but certain spices and herbs can be grouped together.

‣ Strong or dominant flavor : Includes bay leaf, cardamom, curry (actually a blend of spices), ginger, pepper, mustard, rosemary, sage.

- Medium flavors : Use in moderate amounts (1 to 2 teaspoons for 6 servings). Includes basil, celery seeds and leaves, cumin, dill, fennel, French tarragon, garlic, marjoram, mint, oregano, savory, thyme, turmeric.
- Delicate flavors : Includes burnet, chervil, chives, parsley. May be used in large quantities and combined with most other herbs and spices.
- Sweet flavor (combined in sweet dishes may let you reduce sugar) : Includes cinnamon, cloves, allspice, ginger, cardamom, anise, fennel, mint.
- Savory flavor : Oregano, tarragon, chives, dill.
- Peppery flavor : Red pepper, mustard, black pepper, paprika. Use with care since their flavors stand out (approximately 1 teaspoon for 6 servings).

- Consider the flavor of the main ingredient in the recipe. In general, the weaker the flavor of the food, the less seasoning needed to give a satisfactory balanced note in the final product.
- Consider the form that will be used. Dried herbs are stronger than fresh herbs because the chemicals that produce the characteristic flavor are more concentrated. Powdered spices are stronger than crumbled spices since the flavoring chemicals can mix with the food easier. A useful guide is: 1/4 teaspoon powdered = 3/4 to 1 teaspoon dried crumbled = 2 to 3 teaspoons fresh.
- When using fresh herbs, chop the leaves very fine. The more cut surface exposed, the more flavor will be released. Kitchen shears are ideal for cutting

fresh herbs, but a knife can also be used.

- Use whole spices in recipes that require lengthy cooking because there is plenty of time for the flavor to be extracted and spread throughout the food. The flavor of herbs is lost however, by extended cooking, so add them during the last 45 minutes if the recipe calls for long simmering. Another technique is to use part of the herb at the beginning and the remainder later in cooking.

- In quick- or medium-cooking dishes, crush dried herbs first to release some of the oils. Use a mortar and pestle or a rolling pin.

- Add herbs several hours or overnight to cold foods such as dips, cheese, vegetables and dressings. This allows the flavors to blend.

- Be conservative in the amount of an herb used until you are familiar with the strength of it. Start with a pinch. You can always add more, but you can't remove it. The flavor can be extremely objectionable if too much is used.

- To test herb or spice combinations in soups or stews, remove 1/2 cup of food from the pan. Add a large pinch (1/8 teaspoon) of each and stir. Allow to stand at room temperature approximately 10 minutes. Taste. If acceptable, add the combination to the remainder of the recipe.

- For salt reduction, choose the savory or biting spices and herbs, blends and vegetable seasonings. Good choices include black pepper, garlic powder or granules, curry powder, cumin, dill seeds, basil, ginger, coriander, onion, tarragon and oregano.

- When reducing sugar, use the sweet spices. They are appealing in sweet dishes, and the amount of sugar may be reduced because they give the impression of greater sweetness.

- When using more than one herb or spice, do not mix two very strong flavored herbs together. Rather, combine one strong flavored with one or more milder flavored herbs to complement both the stronger herb and the food.

4. Storing Herbs and Spices

Keep herbs and spices in a cool, dry place (not over the range!) and in airtight containers. Store dried herbs in plastic bags, glass jars or stainless steel containers rather than in cardboard. Keep containers out of direct sunlight, which fades the color of the herb and reduces the strength.

Your recipes won't taste good if the spice or herb has lost its flavor. Simply adding more than the recipe calls for won't solve the problem. Check whole spices for freshness once a year by crushing a small amount and sniffing it. The aroma should be fresh and pungent. Use the same method to check ground spices every six months and dried herbs 2 to 3 times a year.

Because spices and herbs are expensive, refrigerating or freezing in airtight containers lengthens their life. The flavor and color will last longer, and refrigeration will reduce the chance of insect infestation. Some spices such as paprika, chili powder and red pepper attract insects.

Note

- Cooperative Extension : The Cooperative Extension System is a nationwide educational network that is a collaboration of federal, state and local governments and a state land-grant university. The mission of the Cooperative Extension System is to disseminate research-based information on topics as varied as nutrition, child rearing, agriculture, horticulture, husbandry, small business and personal finance. Every U.S. state and territory has a central state Extension office at its land-grant university. Each state Extension serves its residents through a network of local or regional offices staffed by professionals in their field.
- Extension (off-campus college program) : courses or facilities provided by a college or university for people who are unable to attend classes on the campus or during scheduled class periods
- interchangeable : able to be exchanged with each other without making any difference or without being noticed
- season : to improve the flavour of savoury food by adding salt, herbs or spices when cooking or preparing it
- temperate : (of weather conditions) neither very hot nor very cold
- tropical : very hot and often combined with a high degree of humidity
- bark : the hard outer covering of a tree
- berry : a small round fruit on particular plants and trees
- poppy : a plant with large delicate flowers, which are typically red, and small black seeds
- counted : to consider somebody or something, or be considered, in a particular way or as a particular thing
- call for : to need or require a particular thing or quality
- savory : pleasing to the sense of taste
- peppery : having a spicy flavour like pepper
- note : The sign of a particular quality or emotion
- shear : a cutting tool with blades like scissors
- extract : to remove or take out something

- mortar : a hard strong bowl in which substances are crushed into a powder by hitting or rubbing them with a pestle (= heavy tool)
- pestle : a heavy stick made of clay, stone or metal, with a thick rounded end, which is used for crushing substances in a mortar (= a small strong bowl) by hitting or rubbing them
- rolling pin : a tube-shaped object that is used for making pastry flat and thin before cooking it
- dips : a cold thick creamy sauce which you eat by dipping pieces of uncooked vegetable or biscuits, etc. into it
- conservative : cautiously moderate and therefore often less than the final outcome
- stand : to remain stationary or inactive
- biting : causing a sharply painful or stinging sensation; used especially of cold
- appealing : attractive or interesting
- complement : to make something else seem better or more attractive when combining with it
- airtight : completely closed so that no air can get in or out
- fade : to (cause to) lose colour, brightness or strength gradually
- infestation : of animals and insects which carry disease) to cause a problem by being present in large numbers

References

Snider, Sue, 2007, "Using Herbs and Spices," 15, Mar., Retrieved Jan. 4, 2010 from http://ag.udel.edu/extension/fnutri/pdf/CookingGuide/fnf-03.pdf

Retrieved Jan. 4, 2010 from http://ag.udel.edu/extension/index.php

Retrieved Jan. 4, 2010 from http://encarta.msn.com/,

Retrieved Jan. 4, 2010 from http://www.merriam-webster.com/,

Retrieved Jan. 4, 2010 from http://dictionary.cambridge.org/,

Chapter 06

The World's Healthiest Foods

You are what you eat! If you take charge of your health by eating knowledgeably, you can have a healthy life. Your immune system can protect you from infectious disease. You can delay the onset of degenerative disease and defy aging. Nourish your body well and it will serve you well much longer.

Among the thousands of different foods our world provides, the majority contains at least several of the nutrients our bodies need, but to be included as one of the World's Healthiest Foods they can serve as the basis of your healthiest way of eating. Thanks to growing interest in international cuisines, it's never been easier to locate the ingredients you need to prepare foods of other cultures. And great news is many of your favorite global ingredients just happen to have great health benefits. A short description on the World's Healthiest Food with reference to their benefits and their availability is presented (Raymond, n.d.). Let's look at them.

1. Olive Oil (Spain)

"We start with olive oil as babies," says Antonio Diaz, a native of Spain and owner of tapas restaurant Costa del Sol in New York. Olive oil is mandatory at every meal in a typical Spanish home, and for good reason: The country makes more than 40 percent of the world's supply, although until recently the majority was sold and packaged outside its borders (the Italian olive oil you're using might actually be from Spain). Spanish olive oil producers are now labeling their own brands, and making a name for themselves as the source for top-quality oil. And with more than 262 different olive varieties (24 of which are used for oil), Spanish oils are more diverse than those from other countries.

1) Why to try it

Antioxidant-rich olive oil protects against heart disease by controlling LDL, or bad, cholesterol levels while raising HDL, or good, cholesterol. In fact, it's such a health boon that the U.S. Food and Drug Administration (FDA) lets olive oil producers put a heart-health claim on their labels. (It's one of a handful of foods to get that blessing.) But new research shows olive oil may be more than just good for your ticker. Scientists from Philadelphia's Monell Chemical Senses Center discovered that olive oil has a compound with the same structure as ibuprofen, the widely used anti-inflammatory painkiller in Advil and Motrin. That means olive oil may offer the same benefits as low doses of the drug, including reduced risk of heart attack, stroke, some cancers, and even Alzheimer's disease. It also may help fight breast and colon cancers.

2) What to do with it

Light and aromatic, Spanish olive oil is easy to find at your local grocery store or online at Tienda.com for about $10 to $20 per 17-ounce bottle. Dunk whole-grain bread in olive oil, or drizzle over grilled vegetables. Or try our Shrimp With Garlic in Olive Oil recipe.

Note

- mandatory : describes something which must be done, or which is demanded by law
- package : ① to put goods into boxes or containers to be sold, ② to show someone or something in an attractive way so that people will like or buy them
- LDL(low-density lipoprotein) : A molecule that is a combination of lipid (fat) and protein. Lipoproteins are the form in which lipids are transported in the blood. Low-density lipoprotein (LDL) transports cholesterol from the liver to the tissues of the body. LDL cholesterol is therefore considered the "bad" cholesterol.
- HDL(High density lipoprotein) : Lipoproteins are combinations of lipids (fats) and proteins. They are the form in which lipids are transported in the blood. The high density lipoproteins transport cholesterol from the tissues of the body to the liver so it can be gotten rid of in the bile. HDL cholesterol is therefore considered the "good" cholesterol. The higher the HDL cholesterol level, the lower the risk of coronary artery disease.
- boon : something that is very helpful and improves the quality of life
- ticker (INFORMAL) : a heart
- compound : a chemical that combines two or more elements
- ibuprofen : A non-steroidal anti-inflammatory drug (NSAID) commonly used to treat pain, swelling, and fever. Common brand names for Ibuprofen include Advil, Motrin, and Nuprin.
- anti-inflammatory : describes a drug that is used to reduce pain and swelling
- Advil : a nonsteroidal anti-inflammatory medicine (trade names Advil and Motrin and Nuprin) used to relieve the pain of arthritis and as an analgesic and antipyretic
- Motrin : a nonsteroidal anti-inflammatory medicine (trade names Advil and Motrin and Nuprin) used to relieve the pain of arthritis and as an analgesic and antipyretic
- stroke : a sudden change in the blood supply to a part of the brain, which can cause a loss of the ability to move particular parts of the body

- Alzheimer's (disease) : a disease that results in the gradual loss of memory, speech, movement, and the ability to think clearly, and that is common esp. among older people
- colon : the lower and larger part of the bowels through which food travels while it is being digested
- dunk : to put (a cookie, bread, pastry, etc.) into a liquid such as coffee or soup for a short time before eating it
- drizzle : dribble liquid over food: to pour very small quantities of a liquid in a thin stream over food

2. Soy (Japan)

A typical Japanese eats soy for breakfast. And lunch. And dinner. "We eat tofu every day," says Mamie Nishide, a cooking instructor and recipe developer who's a native of Nara, Japan. Soybeans, first grown in tropical Asia thousands of years ago, are used in everything in Japan from soy sauce (as ubiquitous as ketchup) to vegetable oil, tofu, and the fermented soybean paste called miso. Japanese eat more soybeans than anyone else, and the long-lived Okinawans top the list at about 60 to 120 grams per person each day, compared with practically zero grams for the average American.

1) Why to try it

Protein-packed soy is high in isoflavones, estrogen-like substances linked to the prevention of cancer and osteoporosis. But its biggest draw may be the dozens of studies showing soy is good for your heart; the FDA even allows certain soy products (with at least 6.25 grams of soy protein per serving) to have a heart-healthy claim on their labels. Plus, some studies have shown that a diet rich in soy can reduce breast-cancer risk. Asian women, for example, have a much lower incidence of the disease compared with their Western counterparts. But other studies suggest that high levels of soy might actually increase breast-cancer risk in women who live in the United States, especially among those with a family history of the disease. (If you have a history of breast cancer or a high incidence in your family, talk to your doctor about how much soy is safe.)

2) What to do with it

Use cooked soybeans instead of garbanzo beans in your next batch of hummus, and add frozen edamame (whole soybeans) to stir-fries. Tofu typically comes in 1-pound blocks for about $1.99 at grocery and health-food stores.

Note

- ubiquitous (FORMAL) : the ubiquity of fast-food outlets (= the fact that they are found everywhere)
- top : outrank all others in something: to be at the head of something such as a list or hierarchy
- isoflavones : Plant compounds found in soy products that can act like a weak estrogen. They are being studied to see if they can help prevent cancer.
- estrogen : Estrogen is a female hormone produced by the ovaries. Estrogen deficiency can lead to osteoporosis.
- osteoporosis : a disease which causes the bones to weaken and become easily broken
- draw : someone or something that a lot of people are interested in
- serving : quantity of food provided: a portion of food, or of a particular type of food, served to one person
- garbanzo bean (US) : chickpea UK : a hard pale brown round bean which can be cooked and eaten
- batch : a group of things or people dealt with at the same time or considered similar in type
- houmous, hummus : a soft smooth savoury food made from crushed chickpeas, oil and lemon juice
- edamame : Fresh green soybeans, typically prepared by boiling in salted water.

3. Yogurt (Greece)

Many think of yogurt as just a sweet snack. But the thick, creamy, rich kind that's traditional in Greece has been integral to Grecians' healthy diet for thousands of years. "We have a custom that before a couple goes on their honey-moon, they eat yogurt with honey and walnuts for prosperity and energy," says Antonios Maridakis, president of Fage USA, importer of Greece's biggest yogurt brand. "A lot of us believe that yogurt is an aphrodisiac."

1) Why to try it

Yogurt promotes intestinal and vaginal health, improves lactose intolerance, builds stronger bones, enhances immunity, lowers blood pressure, and may even have anticancer and weight-loss effects. In a recent study in the International Journal of Obesity, researchers found that obese adults who ate 3 servings of fat-free yogurt a day as part of a reduced-calorie diet lost 22 percent more weight and 61 percent more body fat than those who just cut calories. A plus for Greek yogurt, in particular, is that it doesn't give you the sugar overload of what you usually find in U.S. grocery stores. To save on fat and calories, reach for a low-fat version.

2) What to do with it

Look for Fage Total yogurt at specialty food stores, Whole Foods Market, Wild Oats, and Trader Joe's. A 5-ounce container costs $1.89. Try it with a drizzle of honey and a handful of walnuts or almonds. Or use Greek yogurt in our delicious Grilled Eggplant and Yogurt Dip.

Note

- integral : necessary and important as a part of, or contained within, a whole
- Grecians : A native or inhabitant of Greece
- Fage : FAGE (pronounced "fah-yeh") is the second largest food producer and the leading dairy company in Greece. Through its extensive distribution network, the company sells a wide range of branded dairy products, including yogurt and dairy desserts, milk and milk cream, and cheese. These products are sold under the FAGE® trademark, which is one of the most recognized in Greece.
- aphrodisiac : something, usually a drug or food, which is believed to cause sexual desire in people
- intestinal : located in intestines: found in or affecting the intestines
- vaginal : pertaining to or involving the vagina.
- lactose intolerance : congenital disorder consisting of an inability to digest milk and milk products; absence or deficiency of lactase results in an inability to hydrolyze lactose
- obese : extremely fat

- Fage Total yogurt : Fage사에서 생산되는 요구르트 이름
- Whole Foods Market : Founded in 1980 as one small store in Austin, Texas, Whole Foods Market® is now the world's leading retailer of natural and organic foods, with 192 stores in North America and the United Kingdom. To date Whole Foods Market remains uniquely mission driven: We're highly selective about what we sell, dedicated to stringent Quality Standards, and committed to sustainable agriculture.
- Wild Oats : a natural foods and farmers' market chain of stores in North America.
- Trader Joe's : Just what is this thing we call Trader Joe's? Well, we're a grocery store, sure, but really so much more. Our shelves are stocked full of delicious foods and beverages from the basics like milk, bread and butter to more exotic fare like imported cheeses, organic produce and hand-tossed pizza from Italy. We taste every product before we decide to sell it, and we guarantee you'll like it.

4. Lentils (India)

Lentils are to India as meatloaf is to America: the quintessential comfort food. Ranging from yellow and red to deep black, these tiny disc-shaped members of the legume family are eaten in some form at least twice a day in "any self-respecting Indian household," says Kavita Mehta, founder of the Web-based Indian Foods Co. In fact, India is the world's biggest producer and consumer of lentils. Known as dal, lentils typically are served at every meal with steamed rice or bread.

1) Why to try it

"Superfood" gives you protein and cholesterol-lowering soluble fiber, as well as about twice as much iron as other legumes. And lentils are higher in most B vitamins and folate, which is especially important for women of childbearing age because folate reduces the risk of birth defects. Plus, U.S. Department of Agriculture researchers discovered that the pigment in Beluga black lentils acts like an antioxidant and helps protect against heart disease, cancer, and the aging process in general. Not too shabby for something the size of a pencil eraser.

2) What to do with it

Lentils can be stored a long time, are easy to make, and are one of the cheapest protein sources going, at just 75 cents per pound at grocery stores. And unlike other legumes, you don't have to soak them before cooking. Just rinse them in cold water and simmer in water or broth. Enjoy them plain or spiced with herbs, onions, or garlic.

Note

- meatloaf : a baked loaf of ground meat
- quintessential : being the most typical example or most important part of something
- the legume family : The pea family
- dal : a sauce made from lentils and spices, usually served with rice
- soluble fiber : Dietary fibers are the indigestible portion of plant foods that move food through the digestive system, absorbing water
- folate : Folic acid, one of the B vitamins that is a key factor in the synthesis (the making) of nucleic acid (DNA and RNA)
- birth defects : unhealthy defects found in newborns, often caused by the mother's exposure to environmental hazards or the intake of drugs or alcohol during pregnancy
- pigment : a substance which gives something a particular colour when it is present in it or is added to it
- Beluga black lentils : This is one of the smallest of the lentil family. Shiny black in color and easy to cook. Makes a beautiful garnish, also great in soups and salads. They look like caviar after cooking.
- shabby : not honourable or fair; unacceptable
- going : the condition of the ground for walking or riding etc
- plain : not decorated in any way; with nothing added

5. Kimchi (Korea)

Koreans eat so much of this super-spicy condiment (40 pounds of it per person each year) that natives say “kimchi” instead of “cheese” when getting their pictures taken. The reddish fermented cabbage (and sometimes radish) dish—made with a mix of garlic, salt, vinegar, chile peppers, and other spices—is served at every meal, either alone or mixed with rice or noodles. And it's part of a high-fiber, low-fat diet that has kept obesity at bay in Korea. Kimchi also is used in everything from soups to pancakes, and as a topping on pizza and burgers.

1) Why to try it

Kimchi (or kimchee) is loaded with vitamins A, B, and C, but its biggest benefit may be in its "healthy bacteria" called lactobacilli, found in fermented foods like kimchi and yogurt. This good bacteria helps with digestion, plus it seems to help stop and even prevent yeast infections, according to a recent study. And more good news: Some studies show fermented cabbage has compounds that may prevent the growth of cancer.

2) What to do with it

There's no need to make your own; just pick it up in the refrigerated section of your grocery store or an Asian market for around $4 per 32-ounce jar (Sunja's is one popular brand). You can wake up your morning by scrambling eggs with kimchi, diced tomatoes, and mushrooms. Use it as a wrap filling or to top a baked potato. Or try Spicy Beef and Kimchi Stew, which won our test kitchen's top rating.

Note

- reddish : slightly red in colour
- radish : a small vegetable, usually red or white and round or finger-shaped, which grows underground and is usually eaten raw in salads
- ferment : to (cause something to) change chemically through the action of living substances, such as yeast or bacteria
- hold/keep sth/sb at bay : to prevent someone or something unpleasant from harming you
- Sunja's : Sunja's Oriental Foods Inc.
- test kitchen : America's Test Kitchen, currently in its seventh season, is the most-watched cooking show on public television—more than 2.9 million viewers watch each episode. The show is filmed in the test kitchen of Cook's Illustrated magazine, located just outside Boston.

References

Raymond, Joan, World's Healthiest Foods, Retrieved Jan. 10, 2007 from http://www.health.com/health/article/

Retrieved Jan. 11, 2007 from http://www.americastestkitchen.com/aboutus.asp

Retrieved Jan. 10, 2007 from http://www.americastestkitchen.com/aboutus.asp

Retrieved Jan. 10, 2007 from http://www.traderjoes.com/about_tjs.html

Retrieved Jan. 10, 2007 from http://www.fageusa.com/history.html

Retrieved Jan. 10, 2007 from http://www.wholefoodsmarket.com/company/index.html

Retrieved Jan. 10, 2007 from http://www.wildoats.com/u/about/

Retrieved Jan. 10, 2007 from http://www.medterms.com/

Retrieved Jan. 13, 2007 from http://dictionary.cambridge.org/

Retrieved Jan. 6, 2007 from http://encarta.msn.com/encnet/features/dictionary/

Retrieved Jan. 5, 2007 from http://www.merriam-webster.com/dictionary/

Chapter 07

Dedicated to Lifelong Learning

Transform Lives through Learning!

Lifelong learning has become an essential goal of an enterprising society. More than a skill, it is an attitude that facilitates and promotes learning and training throughout life. The continual change and evolution of society means that people often have to learn new skills and acquire knowledge in order to keep up with the demands at work and at home. Therefore, to be successful in this profession young students need to combine your education and experience for your professional development and acquire the skills and knowledge the culinary industry demands, but it is a lifelong journey and it comes true only through the lifelong learning. Lest's explore it.

1. Culinary Education

1) Culinary certification (or certificate) in culinary arts

With thousands of chefs competing in the job market, it is essential to prove your culinary competency. Many community colleges, junior colleges, technical schools, other institutions of higher education, and other culinary associations offer various certification programs in culinary arts. A certification demonstrates skill, knowledge and professionalism to the culinary industry. With successful completion of the culinary certification program, students earn a certification in culinary arts or a certificate of completion(=achievement). A certificate of achievement requires a commitment of one year if you attend full-time. Many courses are offered so that students can work and attend them part-time (Acfchefs, n.d.; Tmcc, n.d.). But graduation from a well-respected culinary school and experience in well regarded restaurants generally carries more weight than certification (Newfuturesdc, 2009).

2) Associate degree (or Associate's degree) in culinary arts

It is, in short, expressed as two-year college degree. It is defined as a degree earned on completion of a two-year program of study at a community college, junior college, technical school, or other institution of higher education. An associate degree requires a two-year commitment if you attend full-time (Tmcc, n.d.).

3) Bachelor's degree in culinary arts

It is defined as a degree awarded on the successful completion of an undergraduate course at a four-year college or university. This gives students additional experience, education and a competitive edge upon entering into the culinary industry (Bic, n.d.).

In general there are two ways to earn a bachelor's degree in culinary arts. The first way is, after high school, to progress to a bachelor's degree program at a four-year college or university. During the first two years of the program, students follow the curriculum for the Associate degree, and the following two years focus on more advanced techniques, as well as the training in management and leadership.

The second one is to transfer to bachelor's degree programs; upon completion of your associate degrees in culinary arts, and then students transfer to a four-year college or university to complete your junior and senior years of a bachelor's degree in culinary arts.

Note

- enterprising : showing initiative and a willingness to undertake new, often risky, projects
- facilitate : to make possible or easier
- competency : an important skill that is needed to do a job
- keep up with : to remain abreast of something that undergoes continuous change or progress
- come true : to happen as hoped for
- institution : a large and important organization, such as a university or bank
- commitment : something that takes up time or energy, especially an obligation

2. Taking an Overseas Internship

1) Introduction to Culinary Internships

If you're trying to broaden your experiential backgrounds and supplement your academic studies via a hands-on work experience in a hotel or restaurant environment, culinary internships are for you. Depending upon colleges or universities culinary students are often required to complete an internship, "externship", or practicum as part of their programs. Academic credit can be earned for a successful internship. Internships are offered in 3-month, 6-month and 12-month durations. Interns may extend the duration of your internship program beyond six months. The minimum duration is three months and a maximum of eighteen months. Approval from the student's college or university may be required. Most internships are unpaid positions but some pay an hourly rate (Jobs.foursesons, n.d.; Learn4good, n.d.).

2) Internship vs Externship

The term internship is a chance to try out a prospective career and to gain professional work experience related to a student's major or career goal. The internship plan generally involves a student working in a professional setting under the supervision and monitoring of practicing professionals. Internships are administered by the individual organization desiring interns, therefore, their structure and policies will vary. Internships can be paid or unpaid, and the student may or may not receive academic credit for performing the internship (Mills, n.d.;

Emerson, n.d.; Virginia, n.d.; Ipfw, n.d.).

The word externship designs as a one day job shadowing/mentorship experience, but can be extended longer if you choose. It is an opportunity for students to gain understanding of a business, industry, and/or job function, to ask questions, and to observe first hand day to day business operations. Then what is the difference between an Externship and an Internship? An externship is brief, and offer no pay or academic credit. An internship is usually 3-12 months in duration, and can be paid or for credit (Bc, n.d.).

3) Intern Jobs

Interns are typically assigned to entry-level job classifications based on their background and experience, and their stated personal interests. Culinary internships are temporary positions within hotels or restaurants that allow you to gain practical experience by working alongside professionals. Culinary interns will usually be required to concentrate on one area during your internship in which they have a particular interest or expertise. However, some opportunities for cross-training may be available depending on the size of the hotels and restaurants, Culinary interns will rotate through several kitchen stations including the hot line, hot prep, buffets, banquet kitchens, bake shop, and garde manger. Rotation within departments will be based on the student's abilities and desire to excel. The aim of your internship is to learn the policies, systems and procedures in place for each department you work in (Learn4good, n.d.; .Cphiltonhead, n.d.),

4) Benefits

Students interning in hotels or restaurants are encouraged to gain the knowledge, skills and experience that relate directly to your educational program and future career goals. You get the opportunity to apply the knowledge, skills and experience you have gained in real-life situations. This hands-on experience will allow you to make more informed decisions about the career path you take following your graduation (Learn4good, n.d.; .Cphiltonhead, n.d.),.

Many hotels or restaurants that offer culinary internship programs will often give preference to former interns. Former interns are also more likely to be offered a full-time position on graduation as you have had the chance to prove your abilities. Culinary interns in hotels may receive other benefits such as on-site accommodation, free meals or the use of swimming pools or other leisure facilities. But In the U.S., housing, salaries and benefits vary from location to location and will be discussed during the interview process. Culinary internships in hotels or restaurants may be more easily obtained in the busier holiday periods ((Learn4good, n.d.; Jobs.foursesons, n.d.).

On the other hand, throughout the course of your internship, you will find ample opportunities to experience the authentic life of other countries. You will discover the vibrant culture of other countries and meet many people and make friends from all over the world.

Note

- supplement : to add something to something to make it larger or better

- hands-on : relating to, being, or providing direct practical experience in the operation or functioning of something <hands-on training>
- practicum : a period of work for practical experience as part of an academic course
- supervision : when someone watches a person or activity and makes certain that everything is done correctly, safely, etc.
- credit : a unit which represents a successfully finished part of an educational course
- shadowing : the act of following someone secretly
- mentorship : a wise and trusted guide and advisor
- entry-level : at the lowest level and suitable for somebody who is new to a job, field, or subject
- garde manger : ①a cool room used for storing foods and for preparing certain dishes, esp. cold buffet dishes. ② a cook who specializes in the preparation of cold foods (as meats, fish, and salads)
- in place : ready for use
- preference : an advantage which is given to a person or a group of people
- accommodation : a place to live, work, stay, etc. in
- ample : more than enough
- vibrant : energetic, exciting and full of enthusiasm

3. English Interview Tips

1) Tips for a Successful Interview

First impressions matter because they create biases. If you make a bad impression upfront, you will have to combat that bias. It's like running uphill. On the other hand, if you make a good impression, you can ride on it. It's like running downhill (Workbloom, n.d.).

Therefore it is important to make a good initial impression, as recruiters often make up their minds about a candidate within the first few minutes of the interview. To help you make a good impression right from the start, here are a few guidelines for you to follow (Randstad, n.d.):

- Dress professionally.
- Give a firm handshake at the beginning and end of the interview.
- Smile.
- Be confident about yourself and your capabilities.
- Express your motivation and enthusiasm.
- Talk about your achievements, not just your responsibilities.
- Tell the employer about your interest in the job.
- Sit up straight in your chair.
- Ask some questions about the job and the company.
- Be natural, do not try to play a role.
- Make eye contact with the interviewer when answering questions.
- Be spontaneous (even if you've practised for the interview, don't make it seem as though you've memorized all your answers).

2) Frequently Asked Interview Questions

Some of the interview questions which can be frequently asked from you are as follows (Hosko, 2010; Beare, n.d.):

- How are you today?
- Did you have any trouble finding us?
- What do you think of the weather lately?

Don't be surprised by the friendly tone. The interviewer wants to put you at ease or help you relax. Answer the question without going into too much detail. The language you use should be simple but polite, for example;

- How are you doing?

  GOOD : I'm fine thank you, and you? / I'm well thank you.

  BAD : So, so / OK / Not so well

- Tell us about yourself or describe yourself in 3 words?

Well, my name is Joe and I am from Korea. I am at present studying in Hyejeon College.

This is a simple and straightforward answer. It would be better if you adopt this kind of simple answers. From these answers the recruiter will also not be confused and you will be successful as well.

- Why did you apply for our hotel?
- Do you have any information about our hotel?
- Have you been in other countries before?
- Why do you want to work in ________ (country)?
- Could you tell me your previous work experience?
- What did you like the most? What did you like the least?
- Tell me about some of your successes or accomplishments.
- Who is your supervisor?
- Why did you leave your last job?
- Could you tell me about your strengths? / What are your strong points?
- Could you tell me about your weaknesses? / What are your weak points?

- Why do you apply this position?
- Why are you so excited about this job?
- Which position or department do you want to work?
- Would you tell me about your educational background?
- What is your major and favorite class?
- Were you involved in any club or organization at your university?
- What are your interests and hobbies?
- Do you prefer to work alone, or as part of a team?
- What do you expect from this job?
- Why should we hire you?
- What experience / skills do you have that could help us?
- It will be really busy in our hotel. Are you fine with that?
- Will you be able to keep up with this?
- How do you feel about working overtime?
- Do you have goals you want to achieve? What is it?
- Why did you choose your career/ field?
- What would you like to be doing after five years from now? / What position do you expect to have in two years?
- Is there anything you'd like to ask me, anything you're wondering about?

Note

- bias : an unfair preference for or dislike of something
- upfront : frank and honest
- spontaneous : happening or done in a natural, often sudden way, without any planning or without being forced
- keep up with : to remain abreast of something that undergoes continuous change or progress

References

Acfchefs, "Certification Designations," Retrieved Jan. 14, 2010 from http://www.acfchefs.org/Content/NavigationMenu2/Careers/Certification/Designations/default.htm

Acfchefs, "certification," Retrieved Jan. 7, 2010 from http://www.acfchefs.org/Content/NavigationMenu2/Careers/Certification/default.htm

Beare, Kenneth, "Example Job Interview Questions and Answers." Retrieved Feb. 3, 2010 from http://esl.about.com/od/businessspeakingskills/a/job_interview.htm

Bic, "Bachelor of Science in Culinary Management," Retrieved Jan. 7, 2010 from http://www.bic.edu/programs/school-of-culinary-arts/bachelors-degree

Bc, "Externship program," Retrieved Jan. 7, 2010 from http://www.bc.edu/offices/careers/employers/externship.html

Cphiltonhead, "Internship Program," Retrieved Feb. 2, 2010 from http://www.cphiltonhead.com/cp/Career-Opportunities-Internships-Hilton-Head-Island-SC.htm

Emerson, "Internships," Retrieved Jan. 7, 2010 from http://www.emerson.edu/media_arts/VMA-Internships.cfm

Hosko, 2010, "English Interview Tips: Internal materials," Retrieved Feb. 3, 2010 from http://www.hospitalitykorea.com/

Ipfw, "Internships," Retrieved Jan. 7, 2010 from http://www.ipfw.edu/career/students/job/internships.shtml#what

Jobs.foursesons, "Your four seasons future," Retrieved Feb. 2, 2010 from http://jobs.fourseasons.com/Jobs/faq/Pages/FAQs.aspx

Learn4good, "Hotel Internship Programs," Retrieved Feb. 3, 2010 from http://www.learn4good.com/internships/hotel_internship_programs.htm

Mills, "Internships: "General Information," Retrieved Jan. 7, 2010 from http://www.mills.edu/academics/internships/index.php

Newfuturesdc, 2009, 2009-2010 Career Guide; Promising Careers that Don't Require Four Years of College, New Futures, Retrieved Feb. 5, 2010 from http://www.newfuturesdc.org/wp-content/uploads/2009/11/Career-Guide.pdf

Randstad, "Tips for a Successful Interview," Retrieved Feb. 3, 2010 from www.randstad.ca/finding_jobs/successful_interview.aspx

Tmcc, "Culinary Arts Degree and Certificates," Retrieved Jan. 7, 2010 from http://www.tmcc.edu/culinary/degrees/

Virginia, "Internships: Frequently Asked Questions," Retrieved Jan. 7, 2010 from http://www.career.virginia.edu/students/programs/internship/faq.php

Workbloom, "How to Make a Good Impression During Job Interviews," Retrieved Feb. 3, 2010 from http://workbloom.com/interview /how-make-good-impression-during-job-interview.aspx

Retrieved Jan. 13, 2010 from http://encarta.msn.com/

Retrieved Jan. 13, 2010 from http://www.merriam-webster.com/dictionary/

Retrieved Jan. 7, 2010 from http://dictionary.cambridge.org/

Chapter 08

Introduction to Korean Cuisine

Korean food is some of the healthiest on earth, with an emphasis on vegetables, meats cooked simply and without much oil and a near obsession with the fermented vegetable kimchi.

Much of the food that exists today and the customs surrounding it have come from royal cuisine and the complex customs of the ancient court. The food is a study in balance with consideration given to temperature, spiciness, colour and texture along with careful presentation.

1. Korean Food

A diverse array of foods and dishes can be found throughout Korea. Korea was once primarily an agricultural nation, and Koreans have cultivated rice as their staple food since ancient times. These days Korean food is characterized by a wide variety of meat and fish dishes along with wild greens and vegetables. Various fermented and preserved food, such as kimchi (fermented spicy cabbage), jeotgal (seafood fermented in salt) and doenjang (fermented soy bean paste) are notable for their specific flavor and high nutritional value.

The prominent feature of a Korean table setting is that all dishes are served at the same time. Traditionally, the number of side dishes varied from 3 for the lower classes to 12 for royal families. Table arrangements can vary depending on whether a noodle dish or meat is served. Formal rules have developed for table setting, demonstrating the attention people pay to food and dining. Compared to neighboring China and Japan, a spoon is used more often in Korea, especially when soups are served (Chinatownconnection, n.d.).

2. Korean Cooking in America

Until recently, if you had asked the average American to describe Korean food, you'd probably have gotten a blank stare. But this is beginning to change. Growing Korean communities in the U.S. have given rise to a bumper crop of restaurants and groceries offering once-unavailable dishes and ingredients. The "other" Asian cuisine has already won a devoted following of hip tastemakers, including Kill Bill-director Quentin Tarantino, and it's now coming to the attention of mainstream America (Epicurious, n.d.).

1) Chiles, Seafood, and A Love of Beef

Long misperceived as a simple amalgam of Chinese and Japanese influences, Korean food is in fact distinctive in its taste and history. All three cultures share a love of rice, noodles, and soy sauce. But unique to Korean cuisine are the strong, pungent flavors of dishes like kimchi, a highly seasoned side dish of fermented vegetables that gets a fiery kick from chile peppers. Kimchi is ubiquitous in Korean meals.

In this peninsula land, seafood features prominently—a large variety of fish and shellfish are used both fresh and dried. Vegetarian dishes, a remnant of the country's Buddhist heritage, are usually steamed or stir-fried and seasoned with scallions, garlic, sesame seeds, and sesame oil. Barbecued beef, which reflects Mongolian influence, was once reserved for special occasions but now enjoys great popularity due to the wider availability of meat in postwar South Korea.

2) A Healthy Balance

Korean meals are not eaten in courses. Main dishes, sides, and condiments are served family-style with white rice. Cooks strive to harmonize five essential flavors (salty, sweet, sour, hot, and bitter) and colors (green, red, yellow, white, and black) as exemplified in the dish known as bibim bob, a bowl of rice topped with sautéed beef, a medley of colorful vegetables, and a spicy sauce. Nutritional balance is also emphasized.

3) Can I Cook It at Home?

Definitely. Traditional Korean home cooking combines simplicity, healthiness, and comfort, which makes it perfect for everyday eating. We consulted with restaurateur Jenny Kwak, who has made a name for herself serving the dishes she remembers from her childhood. Read on for Kwak's tips and recipes.

Note

- staple : basic or main; standard or regular
- greens : the leaves of green vegetables such as spinach or cabbage when eaten as food
- preserved : to treat food in a particular way so that it can be kept for a long time without going bad
- a blank stare : A blank stare at the most probably from an offensive joke or a fateful truth revealed.
- give rise to : to cause
- bumper : unusually large in amount:
- crop (INFORMAL) : a group of people or things with something in common, that exist at a particular time
- devoted : extremely loving and loyal
- following : group of followers: a group of people who admire or support somebody or something over a period of time
- hip : fashionable
- tastemaker : a person or thing that establishes or strongly influences what is

considered to be stylish, acceptable, or worthwhile in a given sphere of interest, as the arts.

- mainstream : belonging to or characteristic of a principal, dominant, or widely accepted group, movement, style, etc
- amalgam : a combination of parts that create a complete whole
- fiery : describes food which causes a strong burning feeling in the mouth
- kick (INFORMAL) : the strong effect of an alcoholic drink
- remnant : a small piece or amount of something that is left from a larger original piece or amount
- condiment : a substance, such as salt, that you add to food to improve its taste
- exemplify : to be or give a typical example of something
- medley : a mixture of different items, especially tunes put together to form a longer piece of music
- Jenny Kwak : As a small child, Jenny Kwak had dreams of opening a restaurant. Upon finishing college, her dreams finally became a reality. Living in downtown Manhattan, she was very aware of the lack of Korean restaurants in the area: "I thought a Korean restaurant would do well in this part of town because our food is so different. I also wanted my Mom to be the chef of this restaurant. She's very astute, a good businesswoman, and, obviously, a wonderful cook. She also has the innate sensibility of being a mother. She's very accommodating, caring, and nurturing, and this is reflected in her food."

3. Korean Dish 'may cure bird flu'

BBC News reported that South Korea's spicy fermented cabbage dish, kimchi, could help to cure bird flu, according to researchers (Chazan, 2005). Let's read it.

South Korea's spicy fermented cabbage dish, kimchi, could help to cure bird flu, according to researchers. Scientists at Seoul National University say they fed an extract of kimchi to 13 infected chickens—and a week later 11 of them had started recovering.

The researchers said the results were far from scientifically proven and if kimchi did have the effects they observed, it was unclear why.

South Koreans are reported to be eating more kimchi as a result of the study.

"I'm eating kimchi these days because I've heard in the media that it helps prevent bird flu infections," one man said.

Love it or loathe it, once you have eaten it, you will never forget it. Kimchi is made by fermenting cabbage with red peppers, radishes and a lot of garlic and ginger.

The idea that it could help poultry to fight off bird flu sounds like a dubious folk remedy.

But the theory is being floated by some of Korea's most eminent scientists.

"We found that the chickens recovered from bird flu, Newcastle disease and bronchitis. The birds' death rate fell, they were livelier and their stools became normal," said Professor Kang Sa-ouk.

Sars link

There was an increase in kimchi consumption two years ago, when thousands of people in Asia contracted Sars (severe acute respiratory syndrome).

Kimchi was reported to have helped to prevent Sars. The claim was never scientifically proven, but according to some Koreans, people in other countries followed their example and started eating kimchi.

"After the Sars outbreak, I went to China and I noticed that the Korean restaurants there sold most of the kimchi they'd made that day," a Korean man said.

So one of Korea's national specialities may soon find a much bigger market. Whether it really is an effective remedy, only time and more research will tell.

Note

- bird flu : Bird flu is an infection caused by avian (bird) influenza (flu) viruses. These flu viruses occur naturally among birds. Wild birds worldwide carry the viruses in their intestines, but usually do not get sick from them. However, bird flu is very contagious among birds and can make some domesticated birds, including chickens, ducks, and turkeys, very sick and kill them.
- feed : to give food to a person, group or animal
- extract : a substance taken from a plant, flower, etc. and used especially in food or medicine
- far from sth : certainly not something
- loathe : to hate someone or something
- fight off : fend off an attacker: to drive away or resist an attacker
- dubious : thought not to be completely true or not able to be trusted
- folk remedy : Systems of medicine based on cultural beliefs and practices handed down from generation to generation. The concept includes mystical and magical rituals, herbal therapy, and other treatments which may not be explained by modern medicine.
- float (SUGGEST) : to suggest a plan or an idea for consideration
- bronchitis : an illness in which the bronchial tubes become infected and swollen, resulting in coughing and difficulty in breathing
- stool : a simple seat with three or four legs and no back or armrests
- Sars : Severe acute respiratory syndrome. A severe form of pneumonia which appeared in outbreaks in 2003.
- outbreak : a sudden beginning of something, especially of a disease or something else dangerous or unpleasant

References

Chinatownconnection, "Korean food," Retrieved Jan. 8, 2007 from http://www.chinatownconnection.com/korean-food.htm

Chazan, David 205, Korean dish 'may cure bird flu' Monday, BBC News, 14 March, Retrieved Jan. 5, 2007 from http://news.bbc.co.uk/go/pr/fr/-/2/hi /asia-pacific/4347443.stm

Retrieved Jan. 8, 2007 from http://findarticles.com/p/articles/mi_m0JAW /is_2002_Winter/ai_97429322/pg_6/

Retrieved Jan. 8, 2007 from http://www.medicinenet.com/bird_flu/article.htm

Retrieved Jan. 8, 2007 from http://www.epicurious.com/features/going_global /korean/intro

Chapter 09

Introduction to Chinese Cuisine

Chinese cuisine is a term for styles of food originating in the regions of China, many of which have become widespread and popular in other parts of the world — from Asia to the Americas, Australia, Western Europe and Southern Africa. Where there are historical immigrant Chinese populations, the style of food has evolved — for example, American Chinese cuisine and Indian Chinese cuisine are prominent examples of Chinese cuisine that has been adapted to suit local palates. In recent years, connoisseurs of Chinese cuisine have also sprouted in Eastern Europe and South Asia. The culinary Michelin Guide has also taken an interest in Chinese cuisine, establishing Hong Kong and Macao versions of its publication.

from Wikipedia

1. Yin-Yang Foods

The Chinese believe that to achieve bodily harmony, you must balance your intake of yin (cool, bland) foods with yang (the rich and hot). They further believe that winter is yang season (the time for spicy, heavy food) and summer yin; that new mothers should eat yang foods, as should the chronically fatigued. Yin foods, on the other hand, are recommended for the irritable. The Chinese classify ailments as yin (cold) or yang (hot) and believe that as the body ages, it becomes increasingly yin. Such yin diseases as anemia are treated with yang foods, and assorted yang infections (sore throats, measles, etc.) with yin foods.

Not all Chinese agree on which foods are yin or yang, but as a general rule, they break down as follows:

Yin Foods: Bean curd and sprouts, all bland or boiled foods, the cabbage family, carrots and celery, cucumber, duck, some fish and fruits, American ginseng, most greens, honey, melons, milk, pears, pork, potatoes, seaweed and soybean products, white turnips, water and watercress, winter squash, most white foods.

Yang Foods: Bamboo, beef, broiled meats, catfish, chicken and chicken soup, eggs and eggplant, fatty meats and fried foods, garlic and ginger, Korean ginseng, glutinous rice, green peppers, hot and spicy foods, leeks and onions, liquor, mushrooms, peanuts, persimmons, pig's knuckles and pork liver, red foods (beans, peppers, tomatoes, etc.) sesame oil, shellfish, sour foods, tangerines, vinegar and wine (Anderson, Jean and Barbara Deskins, 1995).

2. Chinese Food: History, Popularity, Healthy

Chinese food now holds a popular place among the entire population of the world. You can find a chinese restaurant in every major city and in many smaller areas of the world as well. Let's find out why chinese food is so popular, if chinese food is healthy, and what the history of chinese food is (Chinatownconnection, n.d.).

1) History of Chinese Food

The history of Chinese food is an interesting one. Unlike many cultures the Chinese believe that the preparation of food is an art and not simply a craft. The art of cooking Chinese food can include dishes and food preparation techniques which are difficult to develop and may require the expertise of a chef with lots of experience. One such technique is noodle pulling (scroll down to the bottom of the page to learn more about this technique). Noodle pulling requires skill and lots of practice and results in a delicious noodle dish. This article will refer to noodle pulling later on, but for now, let’s go back to the history of Chinese food.

Chinese food and the way it is prepared is very much influenced by the two major philosophies, which influence the entire Chinese culture. These dominant philosophies are Confucianism and Taoism. Both have these philosophies have influenced the way that the Chinese people cook and the way that they enjoy their food.

2) Confucianism and Chinese Cuisine

Confucius was the man behind the Confucianism beliefs. Among many other standards Confucius established standards for proper table etiquette and for the appearance and taste of Chinese food. One of the standards set by Confucius (you might have noticed this at an authentic Chinese restaurant) is that food must be cut into small bite size pieces before serving the dish. This is a custom that is definitely unique to the Chinese culture.

Knives at the dinner table are also considered to be a sign of very poor taste by those who embrace Confucianism beliefs. The standards of quality and taste that Confucius recommended required the perfect blend of ingredients, herbs and condiments—a blend which would result in the perfect combination of flavor. Confucius also emphasized the importance of the texture and color of a dish, and taught that food must be prepared and eaten with harmony. Interestingly enough, Confucius was also of the opinion that an excellent cook must first make an excellent matchmaker.

3) Taoism and Chinese Cuisine

Those who follow the Taoism beliefs focus on the health benefits of particular foods vs. the presentation of the same. Taoists search for foods that will increase their health and longevity. They search for foods that have healing powers. Many times these benefits were often referred to as 'life giving powers'. For instance, the Chinese found that ginger, which can be considered to be a garnish or a condiment was found to be a remedy for upset stomachs or a remedy for colds.

4) Is Chinese Food Healthy?

Chinese food, when authentic is probably the healthiest food in the world. Some restaurants, which are not authentic, prepare their menu with highly saturated fats or with meats that contain unhealthy amounts of animal fat. These Chinese restaurants are not recommended and they are both neither authentic nor healthy.

Good Chinese food however, is prepared and cooked with poly-unsaturated oils. Authentic Chinese food does not require the use of milk-fat ingredients such as cream, butter or cheese. Meat is used, but not in abundance, which makes it easy for those who love authentic Chinese food to avoid high levels of animal fat. Many believe that authentic Chinese food is really the ideal diet.

Note

- Confucianism : the system of ethics, education, and statesmanship taught by Confucius and his disciples, stressing love for humanity, ancestor worship, reverence for parents, and harmony in thought and conduct
- Taoism : a religion developed originally in ancient China which emphasizes a simple and natural life
- Confucius : Chinese philosopher and teacher
- embrace : to accept something enthusiastically
- upset stomach : a disorder of digestive function characterized by discomfort or heartburn or nausea
- saturated fat : One of the three categories of fatty acids that also includes monounsaturated fats and polyunsaturated fats. This type of fat is primarily derived from animal meat, dairy products and some tropical plant oils, such as palm and coconut. Saturated fat is associated with health risks including heart disease and cancer. Commercially available foods that are high in saturated fat include butter, lard, suet, margarine, vegetable shortening, whole milk, non-dairy whipped cream, meat, cakes, and pastries. Most saturated fats are solid at room temperature.
- poly-unsaturated : describes a fat or oil which has a chemical structure that does not easily change into cholesterol (=a fatty substance that can cause heart disease):

References

Anderson, Jean and Barbara Deskins, 1995, yin yang foods in The Nutrition Bible : The Comprehensive, No-Nonsense Guide to Foods, Nutrients, Additives, Preservatives, Pollutants and Everything Else We Eat and Drink, 1st ed., William (New York; Morrow & Co),

Chinatownconnection, "Chinese Food: History, Popularity, Healthy," Retrieved Jan. 9, 2007 from http://www.chinatownconnection.com/chinese_food.htm

Chapter 10

Introduction to Japanese Cuisine

Japanese cuisine, undoubtedly one of the healthiest and most interesting diets in the world, is renowned for its visual appeal.

Japanese cuisine is known for its three principal virtues such as freshness of ingredients, seasonality of ingredients and simplicity of presentation which are introduced under the title of the characteristics of Japanese cuisine. Back in 2007, in consideration of the global trend in Japanese restaurants, Japan's Ministry of Agriculture, Forestry and Fisheries organized Council of Advisors for the Recommendation of Japanese Restaurants Outside Japan in order to make Japanese Restaurant Recommendation Program. Let's look at it.

1. The Characteristics of Japanese Cuisine

Japanese cuisine is often referred to as the "cuisine of water". If you look at Japan's geography, it's not hard to see why. Surrounded by ocean, the slip of mountainous islands that make up Japan are lined with rivers, and from these abundant waters the Japanese caught fresh fish, the centrepiece of most Japanese meals.

Great importance is placed on the freshness of the fish. And when it comes to vegetables, seasonality is paramount. So freshness and seasonality are the two most important principal virtues of Japanese cuisine.

Simplicity is the third principal virtue of Japanese cooking. Seasonal vegetables are washed and cooked lightly in water, always simply to bring out their subtle flavor. Even dishes that require tedious preparation remain in essence, aesthetically simple.

Japan's neighbours like China, and visitors like the Portuguese introduced new methods of food preparation like frying (e.g. tempura from the Portuguese; the principles of yin and yang which determines food presentation from the Chinese). While that gave Japanese cooking added depth, Japanese cuisine is still principally about water—dashi, (bonito stock) which is made from kombu (seaweed) and bonito flakes in water is the foundation stone of all Japanese dishes. Japanese food then, is essentially, fresh, seasonal flavours cooked simply in water. For this reason, it is wearing the "healthy" tag well (Keiskitchen, n.d.).

Note

- slip (OLD-FASHIONED) : slip of a small and thin, usually because of being young
- centrepiece : the most important or attractive part or feature of something
- tedious : boring
- in essence : relating to the most important characteristics or ideas of something
- yin and yang : Chinese words for complementary and opposite forces that make up the life force
- dashi : Basic soup and cooking stock made with kombu and katsuoboshi.
- bonito : Also known as skipjack tuna
- kombu (kelp) : used in making dashi (soup stock).
- bonito flakes : Bonito flakes are shavings from the dried flesh of the bonito, a fish which is a relative of the mackerel. It is an essential component of Japanese cuisine and one of the key ingredients of the widely used stock called dashi.
- foundation stone (stone beginning construction) : a stone laid during a ceremony to mark the start of construction of a building or institution

2. Japanese Restaurant Recommendation Program (Draft)

Japanese cuisine is an asset to our nation that is revered around the world and has been forged throughout the course of Japan's long history. Sharing Japanese cuisine with the rest of the world will serve not only to improve the image of Japan, but will also allow Japan to contribute to the food cultures and lifestyles of countries around the world.

Japanese cuisine is currently attracting attention from across the globe as a healthy alternative and an ideal dietary lifestyle, and the number of Japanese restaurants around the world is rapidly increasing. These Japanese restaurants are providing people overseas with an opportunity to come into contact with Japanese cuisine and traditional ingredients and also a range of Japanese culture.

Japanese restaurants are also a showroom to present Japanese cuisine to the outside world. At present, Japanese agricultural and marine industries and the food industry of Japan are trying to increase exports and increase their presence in overseas markets in order to expand beyond the well developed and saturated market at home. Japanese restaurants are the first place for foreign people to meet Japanese food and agricultural and marine products. It can be said that it is inevitable to start with restaurants if you intend to penetrate the market abroad with food from Japan.

We are excited at the prospect of more people coming to enjoy Japanese cuisine and the spread of traditional Japanese ingredients around the world as the number of Japanese restaurants increases, and this is the time to accelerate and to evolve this movement.

However at present the number of restaurants is rapidly increasing despite a lack of information concerning Japanese food and without the provision of ingredients that not only characterize, but are essential to Japanese cuisine. As a result, there is a concern that the good reputation of Japanese cuisine could be damaged.

In consideration of this global trend in Japanese restaurants, a range of measures are currently in place including the start of a recommendation program for Japanese restaurants in Paris and the formation of Japanese food-related organizations in countries around the world (MAFF, 2007).

Note

- revered : to very much respect and admire someone or something
- forge : to make or produce, especially with some difficulty
- showroom : an area where merchandise (such as cars) can be displayed
- saturated : completely wet
- penetrate : to move into or through something
- evolve : to develop gradually, or to cause something or someone to develop gradually
- in place : established, instituted, or operational <systems in place>

References

Retrieved Jan. 10, 2007 from http://www.keiskitchen.com.au/sub.jsp?a=1134055691

Ministry of Agriculture, Forestry and Fisheries (MAFF), 2007, "Proposal for Japanese Restaurant Recommendation Program (Draft)," Council of Advisors for the Recommendation of Japanese Restaurants Outside Japan, 6 March, Retrieved Jan. 20, 2010 from http://www.maff.go.jp/e/soushoku/sanki/easia/e_sesaku/japanese_food/pdf/proposal_e.pdf

Chapter 11

Introduction to Western Cuisine

Portrait of Marie Antoine Carême

Western Cuisine is a term used for cuisine in The Americas and in Europe. The Americas (sometimes referred to as America) is the area including the land mass located between the Pacific Ocean and the Atlantic Ocean, generally divided into North America and South America. ... Europe forms the westernmost part of Eurasia. ...

from encyclopedia

1. The Great Chefs

1) Marie Antoine Carême

The first, and in many ways the most important of all French chefs, was Marie-Antoine Carême, who has been called the Architect of the French Cuisine. Marie Antoine Carême was the founder and architect of French haute cuisine.

Carême was born shortly before the Revolution, the 16th child of an impoverished stonemason. When he was only 11, he was abandoned in the street. Fortunately for gastronomy, Carême found his way to an eating house, where he was put to work in the kitchen. Later he moved to a fine pastry shop where he learned not only to cook but also to read and draw.

Carême was employed by the French foreign minister, Charles-Maurice de Talleyrand, who was not only a clever diplomat but a gastronome of distinction. Following his service with Talleyrand, Carême practiced his art for a succession of kings and nobles. He catered a series of feasts for Tsar Alexander of Russia, was chef de cuisine to England's Prince Regent (who later became George IV), and finally was employed by Baroness Rothschild in Paris.

He wrote several voluminous works on cookery, which included hundreds of recipes, menus, history of French cookery, instructions for organizing kitchens, and of course, instructions for monumental architectural constructions of food for pièces montées. He died at the age of 48, and is remembered as the "chef of kings and the king of chefs (Londonfoodfilmfiesta, n.d.)."

2) Auguste Escoffier

He began his long and distinguished professional culinary career at the age of 13 and retired at age 74 after an unprecedented 62-year career, and died at the ripe old age of 89. During his lifetime, he made French cuisine world famous. Escoffier revolutionized and modernized menus, the art and practice of cooking, and the organization of the professional kitchen as well. Three of his cookbooks are still regarded as indispensable references.

He also restructured the kitchen so that it operated as a single integrated unit, a system that prevails today. Escoffier's prestige had the ripple effect of elevating the status of cooks from laborers to artists. Kaiser Wilhelm II once said to Escoffier, "I am the Emperor of Germany, but you are the emperor of chefs." Hotelier Cesar Ritz, whom Escoffier met in 1884, provided not only the stage for the young chef's talents, but also the audience. Ritz's illustrious Savoy and Carlton Hotels' kitchens were headed by Escoffier during an era when the international clientele included the rich, the powerful and the famous. Ritz and Escoffier redefined restaurants and raised hospitality to unparalleled heights.

Escoffier's contributions to culinary art included founding magazines and writing books; the best-known are guides for the modern chef: Le Guide Culinaire (1903), Le Livre des Menus (1912), and Ma Cuisine (1934) (Lesdamesdc, n.d.).

Note

- impoverished : very poor
- stonemason : a person whose job it is to cut, prepare and use stone for building
- gastronomy : the art and knowledge involved in preparing and eating good food
- gastronome : someone who enjoys and knows about high quality food and drink

- distinction : excellence in quality or talent
- succession : a sequence of people or things coming one after the other in time
- Tsar : (until 1917) the male Russian ruler
- pièces montée (set piece) : food that has been decoratively shaped or arranged
- unprecedented : never having happened or existed in the past
- ripe old age : old age
- indispensable : necessary: extremely desirable or useful, or not to be done without
- prevail : to be common among a group of people or area at a particular time
- prestige : respect and admiration given to someone or something, usually because of a reputation for high quality, success or social influence
- ripple effect : a spreading series of effects or consequences caused by a single event
- audience : a group of people assembled to watch and listen to a show, concert, movie, or speech
- illustrious : famous, well respected and admired
- unparalleled : having no equal; better or greater than any other
- found : to bring something into existence

2. Special Expressions in Western Cuisine

1) Haute cuisine vs Nouvelle cuisine

Haute cuisine is defined as cooking of a high standard, typically French cooking. Nouvelle cuisine is defined as a style of cooking in which food is lightly cooked and served in attractive patterns on the plate in small amounts. It is, in a word, the marriage of health-conscious California to traditional France. Consider it an updated version of French cuisine — flavorful food with a light-handed, healthy approach. It's difficult to define nouvelle cuisine in more specific terms because of its huge impact on the way food in general is prepared today. Nouvelle cuisine opened doors to a new generation of restaurant-goers who loved rich tastes and fresh combinations, but didn't want their bodies to pay for it later (Seniorfitness, n.d.; Dictionary.cambridge, n.d.).

2) French paradox

The French paradox is the observation that the French suffer a relatively low incidence of coronary heart disease, despite having a diet relatively rich in saturated fats. The term French paradox was coined by Dr. Serge Renaud, a scientist from Bordeaux University in France in 1992 (Carnaval, n.d.).

3) Master chef

It is a professionally qualified chef who has the title of Certified Master Chef

(C.M.C.)—an honor which is held by less than 100 people in the United States of America. This certification is given out only to those chefs who have received a lot of training and have demonstrated a recognizable level of excellence in intensive 8-day test of culinary skills and knowledge (Culinaryschoolsu, 2009; Acfchefs, n.d.).

On the other hand, this title is called as "Master Craftsman Cook," or 기능장 in Korean whose certification is given out after a test of 60 multiple choice questions on culinary knowledge and 5-hour test of culinary skills (Human Resources Development Service of Korea, n.d.).

4) Celebrity chef

The term celebrity chef applies to a class of chefs who are well known for presenting cookery advice and demonstrations via mass media, especially television (Wikipedia, n.d.). British actor and writer Ian Kelly wrote a biography titled "The Life of Antonin Careme, the First Celebrity Chef" in published in 2004 (Block, 2004). As you can see the title, Ian described Marie Antoine Carême, one of the great chefs in culinary history, as the first celebrity chef.

Note

- paradox : a statement, proposition, or situation that seems to be absurd or contradictory, but in fact is or may be true
- coronary : relating to the arteries (= thick tubes) that supply blood to the muscles of the heart
- saturated fat : a type of fat found in meat, eggs, milk, cheese, etc., which is thought to be bad for your health because it has a chemical structure with no double bonds

- intensive : involving a lot of effort or activity in a short period of time
- celebrity : the state of being famous
- cookery : the skill or activity of preparing and cooking food

References

Acfchefs, "Certified Master Chef®," Retrieved Jan. 13, 2010 from http://www.acfchefs.org/Content/NavigationMenu2/Careers/Certification/Designations/CMC/default.htm

Block, Melissa, 2004, "Antonin Careme: The First Celebrity Chef Biography Highlights Career of a 19th-Century Culinary Star," May 25, Retrieved Jan. 5, 2010 from http://www.npr.org/templates/story/story.php?storyId=1909346

Carnaval, "WINE: The French Paradox," Retrieved Jan. 5, 2010 from http://www.carnaval.com/france/wine/index.html

Culinaryschoolsu, 2009, "Culinary Tools of the Trade," Aug. 25, Retrieved Jan. 13, 2010 from http://www.culinaryschoolsu.com/blog/tag/master-chef/

Human Resources Development Service of Korea, "국가자격종목별상세정보," Retrieved Feb. 5, 2010 from http://www.q-net.or.kr/

Lesdamesdc, "Auguste Escoffier," Retrieved Jan. 6, 2010 from http://www.lesdamesdc.org/index.php?com=aboutus

Londonfoodfilmfiesta, "French Cuisine," Retrieved Jan. 6, 2010 from http://www.londonfoodfilmfiesta.co.uk/FILMMA~1/French%20Cuisine.htm

Seniorfitness, "What is Nouvelle Cuisine?," Retrieved Jan. 5, 2010 from http://www.seniorfitness.com/tutorials/What_is_Nouvelle_Cuisine_396372_Nutrition_article.html

Retrieved Jan. 13, 2010 from http://encarta.msn.com/

Retrieved Jan. 13, 2010 from http://en.wikipedia.org/wiki/Celebrity_chef

Retrieved Jan. 13, 2010 from http://www.macmillandictionary.com/dictionary/british

Retrieved Jan. 13, 2010 from http://www.merriam-webster.com/dictionary/

Retrieved Jan. 7, 2010 from http://dictionary.cambridge.org/

Retrieved Feb. 5, 2010 from http://www.statemaster.com/encyclopedia/

Chapter 12

Introduction to Food Service Management

The food service industry is fast becoming the biggest service industry in the world.

1. Menu Trends in 2010

NRA announced that what will be 'Hot' in 2010. NRA's predictions form the foundation of making a wise decision in culinary industry. Let's look at it (Qsrmagazine, 2009),

The National Restaurant Association's annual survey of more than 1,800 professional chefs — members of the American Culinary Federation (ACF) — reveals that local sourcing of ingredients, sustainability, and nutrition will be the hottest trends on restaurant menus in 2010. Locally grown produce, locally sourced meats and seafood, sustainability, mini-desserts, and locally produced wine and beer top the list of nearly 215 culinary items in the "What's Hot in 2010" survey. Rounding out the top 10 trends are nutritious kids' meals, half-portions, farm-branded ingredients, gluten-free/food-allergy conscious meals, and sustainable seafood.

"No one has a better view of restaurant menu trends than the chefs of the nation's nearly one million restaurants, and that is why we survey these culinary professionals on what hot, new trends we'll see in the coming year," says Dawn Sweeney, president and CEO of the Association. "The top trends this year — local sourcing, sustainability, and nutrition — reflect wider societal trends and consumers' growing interest in these issues. Many restaurants are sourcing some of their ingredients locally, and you often see chefs shopping at farmer's markets to create a host of better-for-you options that today's diners want."

Michael Ty, national president of ACF, agrees. "This is retro — it's what we did in the past when chefs relied on local markets because we did not have the luxury of today's transportation system. We are going back to our roots and the foundation of our craft that made it more pleasurable."

The Association surveyed 1,854 American Culinary Federation member chefs in October 2009, asking them to rate 214 individual food/beverage items, preparation methods, and culinary themes divided into categories as a "hot trend," "yesterday's news," or "perennial favorite" on restaurant menus in 2010.

The leading culinary theme revealed by the survey is sustainability, which is ranked as the third hottest trend. Whether applied to produce, meat, seafood, or alcoholic beverages, the concepts of environmentally friendly practices and local sourcing—farm-to-fork—are appealing to both restaurant operators and consumers for several reasons, including freshness, minimal transportation, and supporting local communities and businesses. Nutrition is another culinary theme that ranks high on the list of trends at number 15. Healthful options for children, produce, superfruits, bite-size and half portions, and food allergy conscious and gluten-free meals all rank in the top 20, illustrating that consumer interest in health and nutrition continues to grow and that restaurants are responding.

Other menu trends in the top 20 include farm-/estate-branded ingredients, regional ethnic cuisine, non-traditional fish (including barramundi and Arctic char), and newly fabricated cuts of meat (including Denver steak and pork flat iron). Simplicity as a culinary theme and smaller portions for a smaller price are also menu trends for 2010, reflecting the shift in consumer preferences toward value and comfort during the economic downturn.

When it comes to the drink menu, locally produced wine and beer is the fifth hottest trend on the What's Hot in 2010 survey. Other alcohol items in the top 20 chef-rated menu trends include culinary/savory cocktails and artisan liquor.

Topping categories within the survey are: amuse bouche and mini-burgers/sliders in appetizers; quinoa and braised vegetables in side items/starches; ethnic-inspired and traditional ethnic items in breakfast/brunch; bite-size desserts and artisan/house-made ice cream in desserts; regional and fusion in ethnic cuisines; artisan cheeses and black garlic in ingredients; and specialty iced tea and organic coffee in nonalcoholic beverages.

In the preparation methods category, liquid nitrogen freezing/chilling was ranked as the number-one trend, followed by braising, sous vide, smoking, and oil-poaching/confit.

Also included in the survey were questions about kitchen and concept trends. The chefs rated environmentally friendly equipment as the top kitchen equipment trend, and the hottest restaurant concept in 2010 as restaurants with gardens.

When it comes to sources for trendy food and beverage ideas, the chefs ranked television, trade shows, and independent restaurants as the best places to get inspired.

Note

- prediction : when you say what will happen in the future
- the American Culinary Federation (ACF) : The American Culinary Federation, Inc. (ACF), a professional, organization for chefs and cooks, was founded in 1929 in New York city by three chefs' organizations: the Societe Culinaire Philanthropique,

the Vatel Club and the Chefs de Cuisine Association of America. Since our inception, little has changed in our principal goals. We are an organization based on promoting the professional image of American chefs worldwide through education of culinarians at all levels.

In 1976, ACF forever changed the culinary industry by elevating the position of the executive chef from service status to the professional category in the U.S. Department of Labor's Dictionary of Official Titles.

Since this change, the culinary industry and our organization have grown tremendously. In fact, ACF is the largest professional chefs organization in North America. We are made up of more than 22,000 members that belong to more than 230 chapters in four regions across the U.S.

We offer culinary competitions, certification, national apprenticeship program, regional and national events, magazines and much more to help foster the growth of professional chefs and the foodservice industry.

- round out : to achieve a more complete or satisfactory form, or cause something to achieve this
- a host of : a large number of something
- retro : similar to styles, fashions, etc. from the past
- perennial : lasting a very long time, or happening repeatedly or all the time
- farm-to-fork : Relating to the human food chain, from its production to its consumption. Also: farm to fork, from the farm to the fork
- superfruit : It refers to a fruit which combines exceptional nutrient richness and antioxidant quality with appealing taste that can stimulate and retain loyalty for consumer products.
- and that : In addition; besides
- gluten-free : without wheat, rye, barley, buckwheat, or oats or related products
- estate : an area of rural, privately owned property that includes a large residence
- barramundi : large edible Australian lungfish having paddle-shaped fins
- arctic char : a fish of the salmon family, similar to a trout. Native to: northern hemisphere

- downturn : a reduction in the amount or success of something, such as a country's economic activity
- artisan : skilled craftsperson: somebody who is skilled at a craft
- amuse bouche : any small bite of food or appetizer-sized portion, often served before a meal; also called amuse-gueule
- quinoa (S American plant) : a plant of the goosefoot family that is cultivated for its seeds, which are ground and eaten.
- starches : a foodstuff that contains a large amount of starch
- sous vide : the technique of cooking ingredients in a vacuum-sealed plastic pouch, usually for a long time at a low temperature
- oil-poaching : A "trade secret" used by many restaurants to give the meat a more tender texture, oil poaching (also called velveting) seals in the juices of the meat. After marinating, heat between 2—4 cups of oil in the wok to a temperature of about 325 degrees Fahrenheit, and immerse the marinated meat in the hot oil for several seconds. Remove the meat from the wok, drain, and cook further as called for in the recipe.
- confit : meat such as goose, duck, or pork that has been cooked and preserved in its own fat
- inspire : to arouse a particular feeling in somebody

2. A Partial List to Control Expenses

To successfully run a restaurant, restaurant operators including employees should consider many things. One of those things is to control expenses. Controlling expenses is the key of restaurant management. Let's take a look at the article (McVety and McVety & Associates, 2009).

There is no doubt that these are challenging times for all of us in the food service business and for almost all businesses in general. And as I write this article about ways to control expenses, I hope as you review this list, you also make a list of how to increase revenue. My philosophy is that you can reduce/control expenses and put yourself out of business, but if you work to generate more revenue and control (or even reduce) expenses, then you have the best of both worlds and will enjoy a longer business life.

As noted in the title, what follows is only a partial list of ways to control your expenses. I am providing this list to get you started on your own list which should be a lot longer and in more detail. Just remember that you do not want to make any expense changes that will impact *Customer Service and/or Quality of Products*.

So here is the partial list by category:

MEATS:

- Use meat logs, production sheets and thermometers.
- Do not over order.
- Weigh in meats and check against order sheet.
- Have your ovens calibrated.
- Use portion scales and portion properly.
- Pre-portion all sliced meats.
- Make gravies from stock, not bases.
- Do not roast a day ahead.

STOREROOM AND FREEZER:

- Put frozen items away immediately.
- Do not accept partially thawed frozen products.
- Keep storeroom door(s) locked.
- Lock walk-ins and freezers at night.
- FIFO at all times.
- Use frozen eggs when possible.
- Keep inventories to a minimum.

BEVERAGES:

- Do not over produce coffee.
- Check the brix on soda and juice machines daily.
- Lock up coffee in secure storage area.
- Value price soft drinks and other beverages.
- Lock juice and soda machines at night.

PRODUCE:

- Use fresh fruits in season.
- Serve cut fruit rather than whole.
- Do not use pre-packaged salads.
- Utilize leftover fruits and vegetables in salads.

- Use ripest tomatoes and fruits first.
- Merchandise lower cost salads.
- Use outer leaves of lettuce as underliners.
- Order partial cases when smaller quantities are needed.

BAKERY:

- Do not over order.
- Learn bakery codes and monitor freshness of bread and bun deliveries.
- Properly rotate stock daily.
- Prepare own pies when possible.
- Substitute homemade biscuits and cornbread for more costly rolls.
- Cut cakes as needed and not in advance.

LABOR:

- Use job routine and flow chart to improve efficiencies.
- Schedule only those hours needed.
- Eliminate overtime.
- Use part-time staff whenever possible.
- Keep your employees informed-regular meetings.
- Schedule frequent In-service training for all areas.
- Clean as you go.

- Encourage and reward employee suggestions.

REDUCE SUPPLY EXPENSES:

KITCHEN:

- Have a preventive maintenance program.
- Control knives.
- Keep knives sharpened.
- Turn off equipment not being used.
- Set an example by turning off lights in areas not in use, i.e.-walk-ins

PHONE:

- Look for alternative sources for phone service.
- Check your monthly phone bill.
- Use only 800 numbers whenever possible.

LAUNDRY:

- Secure all laundry supplies and requisition out.
- Spot check bundles when delivered.
- Purchase and use rag remnants when possible.
- Don’t pay for loss linen.
- Don’t use aprons for towels.
- Provide lockers with locks for each employee.

- Consider owning and washing your own laundry.
- Issue out disposable cloths, don't just leave an entire box out.

JANITORIAL:

- Take advantage of quantity and drop shipped purchases.
- Regularly monitor all dispensing equipment.
- Use vendor representative to train staff on proper techniques of use and cleaning the dish machine.
- Use the proper product for each cleaning job.
- Use clear garbage bags.
- Don't use aerosol cans when non-aerosol is available.
- Follow directions for pre-mixing any concentrated chemicals.
- Chart soap and jet spray usage and monitor regularly.
- Keep all paper supplies up off the floor and in a secure area.
- Check napkin dispensers—are they dispensing one at a time?
- Are you using the right size napkin?
- Put paper towels in a dispenser, not left on top of it.
- Keep paper supplies to a minimum.
- Limit sizes of cups, lids, etc.
- Make sure the proper can liners are used.
- Lock up trash can liners.

CHINA:

- Check trash cans regularly for china and silverware.
- Put up a chart in the kitchen to advise staff on how much broken china costs.
- Use rubber mats on floors in areas where china is used to prevent breaking if dropped.
- Inventory tableware at least annually.
- Buy smart, do not overstock on china, silverware.

You may think this list is too long to use, but I can tell you it is less than half of what my entire checklist encompasses. Actually, you may want to add to this list categories and/or items that are essential to your business and need to be regularly checked for costs.

Share this list with your staff (communications) and explain the reason and value of having such a list and why all of these items need constant monitoring. Monitoring this list of items can save you money and for your staff, it should not be too difficult to get them involved. If properly trained, your staff should be monitoring all of these items as part of their work routine.

Keeping cost down will help you keep the doors open. As business picks up again and assuming you keep this list and controls in place, you will discover addition profit.

Note

- out of business : not or no longer trading or operating as a business
- log : a full written record of a journey, a period of time, or an event
- sheet : a piece of paper with something printed on it

- thermometer : a device used for measuring temperature, especially of the air or in a person's body
- calibrated : marked with or divided into degrees
- FIFO : first in, first out
- brix : A scale used to measure sugar content of grapes & wine. Each degree of Brix is equivalent to 1 gm. of sugar /100 gm. of grape juice. This is the usual method of determining the alcohol potential of unfermented juice or must.
- merchandise : to encourage the sale of goods by advertising them or by making certain that they are noticed
- job routine : a break down of everything a person has to do for a given shift
- eliminate : to remove or take away
- in-service : happening during your time at work
- Clean as you go (CAYG) : It means to clean things as soon as possible—particularly when cooking—so that you don't have a large amount of cleaning to do when the task is completed. It also means that the workspace is tidier, and that fewer utensils are used.
- 800 number : a toll-free telephone number for long-distance calls that is prefixed by the number 800
- requisition : a necessity (a requirement)
- spot check : sample or investigate quickly or at random
- bundle : a number of things that have been fastened or are held together
- remnants : a small piece or amount of something that is left from a larger original piece or amount
- issue : to supply or distribute something officially
- janitorial : one who keeps the premises of a building (as an apartment or office) clean, tends the heating system, and makes minor repairs
- drop ship : It is where the seller/retailer of a product ships the product directly from the manufacturer to the customer without requiring inventory carrying by the seller/retailer
- jet spray : It is to spray water on a particular area of your cloth.

- on top of sth : in addition to something, especially something unpleasant
- can liner : used for garbage, trash or waste bags. Used in industrial, institutional, office and medical applications
- dustbin bag noun (also dustbin liner) (US garbage/trash bag, also trash can liner) : a plastic bag put inside a dustbin to hold the waste and keep the container clean
- silverware : objects, especially knives, forks, spoons, etc., made of silver
- advise : to tell somebody about something
- encompass : to include, especially different types of things
- assuming (that) : accepting as true without question or proof

3. The Dangers of Eating Fast Food

This article, "The Dangers of Eating Fast Food" published by THE HEART LINKS PROJECT, is to create an environment that supports the development of healthy eating habits and to show how parents and educators cope with the problems of fast food in increasing awareness regarding the negative effects of fast foods. Thus young students need to perceive the several problems coming from fast food (Heartlinks, n.d.). Let's look at it.

In a society that functions at a high speed, fast food has quickly been adopted as the preferred food of choice. Fast food restaurants and their advertisements are permeating our neighborhoods, schools, television, and culture. Burger King and Big Mac burgers have become defining foods of the typical American diet. Corporate goals aim to make these chains more geographically accessible, adding more and more chains to our neighborhood streets.

McDonald's and Burger King are not the only fast food industries invading our communities, our minds, and our stomachs; Taco Bell, Pizza Hut, Kentucky Fried Chicken are just a few others. These industries are successful because they offer consumers a quick, cheap, convenient and tasty meal that is all too often high in fat and salt content and low in fiber and calcium.

Creative marketing strategies that offer super-value meals or super-size perks result in further promotion of these industries. Unhealthy processed foods such as these are a potential health threat since they contribute to the increased prevalence of obesity and chronic disease among Americans. Obesity is becoming the largest public health concern as we enter the new millenium, especially among children.

Obesity increases the risk for high cholesterol and fatty streak development, which translates into greater risk for cardiovascular disease. One meal at a fast food restaurant may contribute a significant amount of fat and sodium for the day. For example, McDonald's new Spanish omelet bagel contains 710 calories, 40 grams of fat, 275 mg of cholesterol and 1,520 mg of sodium. High fat diets and bigger portions in combination with decreased physical activity play major roles in the obesity epidemic.

Technology has its drawbacks since fewer children are playing basketball and the majority of them "surf the net" instead. Children consuming diets high in fat often displace nutrient dense foods such as whole grains, fruits and vegetables. Diets high in fat are also typically low in fiber because of the lack of complex carbohydrates. Complex carbohydrates are often high in fiber, which is associated with lower cholesterol levels, improved digestive function, and decreased risk of cardiovascular disease and some forms of cancer.

Some studies have shown that increasing dietary fiber among children may be preventative in the development of childhood obesity. Unfortunately fast foods are more palatable, more filling and more caloric per bite, resulting in greater demand and increased consumption. Fast food also has many social implications, often acceptable in peer environments or associated as rewards or celebratory meals.

The high salt content of fast foods also pose many threats to the health of Americans, young and old. Salt consumption is associated with high blood pressure, strokes, and kidney function. In addition, some studies have shown that calcium competes with sodium. In other words, as the intake of sodium increases, there is an increase in the urinary excretion of calcium. This increased excretion of calcium may be responsible for reduced peak bone mass and increased bone demineralization which, in turn, increases the risk for osteoporosis and bone fractures among women. This concept is extremely important when thinking in terms of children who are in the critical stage of developing bone density.

The recommended limit for sodium is 2,200 mg. On average, however, women consume 3,200 mg per day. Exceeding these recommendations is often easy since a Burger King Whopper contains 870 mg of sodium and a large order of McDonald's fries contains 290 mg, making it possible for individuals to reach more than half the limit in one meal. On the other hand, the RDA for calcium is 800 mg per day but the average intake among women is less than 600 mg. This information illustrates the need for healthy food alternatives. Incorporating nutrient dense food choices and healthy snacks into an active lifestyle may help improve health of the general population and prevent the onset of disease.

It is apparent that fast foods are always a temptation because they are widely available, convenient and cheap, but as parents and educators it is important to set examples for children to emulate. Parents and educators can be more involved in increasing awareness regarding the negative effects of fast foods and discourage children from consuming them. Since many food patterns begin during childhood, parents and teachers should avoid using fast foods as rewarding meals and attempt to educate children on healthy food choices.

Super-sizing meals to get more for your dollar may contribute to unnecessary calories and fat. Encouraging the consumption of a balanced diet, high in complex carbohydrates such as legumes, fruits, vegetables, and whole grains may result in many health benefits. In addition, promoting a diet rich in calcium, which is found in dairy sources such as low-fat milk and cheese or in other sources such as broccoli or kale promotes peak bone mass and decreased risk for osteoporosis and bone fractures later in life. In general, a diet low in fat, especially saturated fat, low in salt and high in fiber and calcium can prevent obesity and disease.

Advocating nutrient dense diets, rich in whole grains, fresh fruits, and vegetables and increased physical activity may serve as the greatest investment of society, the health of our youth. Parents and teachers can educate and empower children by involving them in creating simple, fun, and creative homemade alternatives. Teaching children skills such as grating cheese, washing and cutting vegetables, may make them more apt to preparing meals themselves, and less likely to purchase fast foods.

Some ideas are baked potatoes, which are a good source of potassium, iron and vitamin C. They can be topped with low-fat sour cream, reduced fat cheese and steamed vegetables such as broccoli. Another idea is homemade pizza made with pita bread, tomato sauce, grated low fat cheese, and fresh vegetables. Other ideas are turkey burgers made with lettuce, low fat cheese and mayonnaise or burritos made with baked beans, low-fat cheese, and vegetables. The ultimate message is that nutritious meals can be fun and can be incorporated into everyday life. Showing children how to prepare low fat snacks and meals may deter them from developing unhealthy eating patterns and prevent the onset of obesity and disease.

Note

- Heart Links : This was founded in 1993, is a project funded by the New York State Department of Health, Healthy Heart Program located at Stony Brook University in the Department of Family Medicine. Comprised of a team of dedicated Registered Dietitians and other public health professionals, the Heart Links staff focuses on recruiting school districts interested in improving the school food environment and working with key district personnel in achieving that goal.
- cope : to deal successfully with a difficult situation
- function : to work or operate
- permeate : to spread through something and be present in every part of it
- defining : giving a distinctive character to something or encapsulating its character
- perk : a benefit given to an employee in addition to a salary, e.g. the use of a car or membership in a club
- prevalent : widespread in a particular area at a particular time.
- obesity : more than average fatness
- chronic : (especially of a disease or something bad) continuing for a long time
- epidemic : a particular problem that seriously affects many people at the same time

- cardiovascular : relating to the heart and blood vessels (= tubes that carry blood around the body)
- drawback : a disadvantage or the negative part of a situation
- displace : to force something or someone out of its usual or original position
- palatable : describes food or drink that has a pleasant taste
- filling : leaving somebody with the feeling of having eaten enough
- implication : the effect that an action or decision will have on something else in the future
- peer : somebody who is the equal of somebody else, e.g. in age or social class
- associated : connected
- celebratory : used for celebrating
- pose : to cause something, especially a problem or difficulty
- stroke : sudden change in the blood supply to a part of the brain, which can cause a loss of the ability to move particular parts of the body
- excrete : to get rid of material such as solid waste or urine from the body
- peak bone mass : the amount of bony tissue present at the end of the skeletal maturation
- bone mass : the mineral content of bone.
- demineralization : elimination of mineral or organic salts from tissues of the body
- osteoporosis : a disease which causes the bones to become weaker and easily broken
- RDA (recommended daily allowance) : the amount of a substance, such as a vitamin, that should be in your food every day
- the onset of sth : the moment at which something unpleasant begins
- emulate : to copy something achieved by someone else and try to do it as well as they have
- legume : a plant that has its seeds in a pod, such as the bean or pea
- advocate : to publicly support or suggest an idea, development or way of doing something
- empower : to give someone official authority or the freedom to do something
- pita bread (UK pitta bread) : flat hollow bread in an oval shape

- burrito : a type of Mexican food made by folding a tortilla (= thin round bread) and putting meat, beans and cheese inside it
- deter : to discourage somebody from taking action or prevent something from happening, especially by making somebody feel afraid or anxious

References

Heartlinks, "The Dangers of Eating Fast Food, THE HEART LINKS PROJECT: A MEMBER OF THE NYS HEALTHY HEART COALITION," Retrieved Jan. 7, 2010 from http://www.stonybrook.edu/heartlinks/fastfooddangers.pdf

McVety, Jerry and McVety & Associates, 2009, "A Partial List to Control Expenses," Food Service and Hospitality Consulting, Retrieved Jan. 7, 2010 from http://www.vending.org/pdf/2009_Control_Foodservice_Expenses.pdf

Qsrmagazine, 2009, "NRA Announces What It Thinks Will Be 'Hot' in 2010," Dec., Retrieved Jan. 6, 2010 from http://www.qsrmagazine.com/articles/news /story.phtml?id=9779

Retrieved Jan. 6, 2010 from http://www.acfchefs.org/Content/NavigationMenu2 /About/Overview/default.htm

Retrieved Jan. 6, 2010 from http://encarta.msn.com/,

Retrieved Jan. 6, 2010 from http://www.merriam-webster.com/,

Retrieved Jan. 6, 2010 from http://dictionary.cambridge.org/,

Chapter 13

Introduction to Food Styling

Food styling is the art of preparing food to be photographed or filmed.

A food stylists is a make-up artist for food.

Most young students interested in the culinary arts choose to work in the kitchen as a chef, while there are a few students who are interested in the more unusual culinary careers that are out there. One of those careers is being a food stylist. If you want to be a food stylist, you have to combine artistic vision with culinary skills. Most of this article is based upon "The Art of Food Presentation: Being a Food Stylist" (CulinarySchools, n.d.). Let's look at it.

1. Things that Food Stylists do

Food stylists combine culinary arts and science to prepare food for thousands of images for print advertisements, television and internet commercials, magazines, cookbooks, health publications, newspapers, food packaging, satellite media tours, talk show presentations, and also for fine art photography and films whether in studio or on location (KarenTemple, n.d.). They are responsible for finding unusual ingredients and preparing food so it looks freshly made and appetizing. A culinary school degree is a must for a food stylist, as the job requires extensive knowledge of how food acts, both aesthetically and scientifically.

2. Tricks that Food Stylists perform

Food stylists know that looks are more important than taste during a photo shoot, and they use culinary tricks to make food the star of the show. For instance, they might substitute heavy cream for milk when photographing cereal as heavy cream looks much more appetizing.

Here are some other tricks of the trade (Liketocook, n.d.).

- Adding aspirin powder to champagne to create extra fizz.
- Sprinkling talcum powder over charcoal to simulate ash
- Injecting some mashed potatoes under the skin of chicken to give chicken that perfect drumstick
- Punching swiss cheese with straws to add holes
- Applying lipstick on strawberries to deepen their redness
- Using hair dryers to cook a slice of turkey
- Using shortening mixed with sugar to simulate ice cream
- Spraying with hair spray to keep cakes look fresh
- Spraying with spray deodorant to give fruits a frosty look
- Spraying with fabric protector to prevent syrup from soaking in pancakes
- Painting with glycerin to look seafood juicy
- Tossing with liquid glucose to give spaghetti that sheen
- Using motor oil instead of syrup

With the advent of digital photography, the food stylist's job has gotten much easier. No longer does the stylist need to worry about such details as the food sitting under the hot lights for hours and hours—photos are now taken and assessed much more quickly.

3. Job Education & Training that Food Stylists receive

Some culinary schools offer styling classes to get you prepared for real-life situations. A love of baking and cooking is a major plus in this field. A good food stylist starts out with a solid culinary education, and spends several years working as a traditional chef before working in the field. The best way to break into the market is to work as an assistant to a professional food stylist, and then branch out into having your own clients. This is a great way to get a feel for the culinary industry and to learn invaluable tricks of the trade. A few years of assistant work can open all sorts of doors for you. It often takes time to break into the market and become a food stylist, so it's important to be as flexible as possible. Do whatever work comes your way, and be willing to go where the work is. Food stylists can earn anywhere from $450 to $850 a day once they are established.

Note

- satellite media tours : Satellite media tours consist of a sequence of one-on-one satellite interviews with a series of pre-booked television reporters across the country or around the world. Satellite media tours typically involve an interview with an author, performer, executive or other spokesperson promoting an upcoming event, product, movie or book release. Satellite media tours generally are conducted from a studio but can originate from remote locations and may be aired live by the television station or recorded for a later airing. Radio media tours are similar to Satellite media tours, but are targeted to radio stations.
- aesthetical : concerning or characterized by an appreciation of beauty or good taste
- substitute : to use something or someone instead of another thing or person
- the trade : the people who work in a particular business or industry or in the same one

- fizz : bubbles of gas in a liquid
- talcum powder : a powder, usually having a pleasant smell, put on the skin to make it feel smooth or to help it stay dry
- inject : to force a liquid or gas through a small opening into a confined space
- drumstick : the lower part of the leg of a chicken or similar bird eaten as food
- deodorant : a substance that you put on your body to prevent or hide unpleasant smells
- frosty : very cold, with a thin layer of white ice covering everything
- fabric protector : This provides a protective barrier on the fabrics. After treatment, spills and stains cannot penetrate the fabrics.
- advent : the arrival of an event, invention or person
- break into sth : to suddenly begin to do something
- branch out : to start to do something different from what you usually do, especially in your job
- anywhere from A to B : used to indicate an approximate measurement of something by giving the smallest and largest possible measurements

References

Culinaryschools, "The Art Of Food Presentation: Being A Food Stylist," Retrieved Jan. 20, 2010 from http://www.culinaryschools.com/being-a-food-stylist

Retrieved Jan. 20, 2010 from http://www.liketocook.com/50226711 /food_stylist_tricks.php

Retrieved Jan. 20, 2010 from http://foodstylist.com/

Retrieved Jan. 13, 2010 from http://dictionary.cambridge.org/

Retrieved Jan. 6, 2010 from http://encarta.msn.com/encnet/features/dictionary/

Retrieved Jan. 5, 2010 from http://www.merriam-webster.com/dictionary/

Chapter 14

Introduction to Wine

Wine is a growth industry.

1. Wine Production and Consumption

1) Wine production

Despite deteriorating global economic conditions, world demand for wine is likely to ease only marginally in 2009 as consumers shift to lower cost brands rather than significantly reduce their consumption. Larger stocks will partially offset lower production, so prices should not change significantly (Office of Global Analysis, 2009).

World wine production stands every year at around 270 million hl (hectoliter), enjoys slight but constant growth thanks to investments by new producer countries and is characterized by significant evolution although Europe still maintains its leadership. Emerging countries are coming to the fore and gaining increasing quotas on international markets, while traditional producers including Italy nevertheless are consolidating their positions, are actively seeking new clients. and are attempting to perfect strategies to avoid losing further ground (Anonymous, 2005).

The leading wine producing countries, Italy, France, Spain, Argentina, and Australia all showed a decrease while USA, China, Germany, South Africa and Chile saw production increases from 2004 to 2008 (See Table 14-1).

Even though wine production in the leading European countries has fallen, Italy, France, and Spain remain the largest producers. The overall share of the European countries listed is falling gradually, from 69.5% in 2004 to 65.6% in 2008.

As can be seen by the final column, there is significant variation in wine production per hectare. Some of this variation is explained by the fact that not all grape production goes into wine. But the variation is the result of differences in production efficiencies, climate, and soil.

Table 14-1 Wine Production by Country and per Hectare

Country	Wine Production ('000 hl)					% Change in Production	2008 (per hectare)
	2004	2005	2006	2007	2008		
Italy	49,935	50,566	52,036	46,600	46,900	-6.1%	56
France	57,386	52,105	52,127	45,800	42,950	-25.2%	50
Spain	42,988	37,808	38,137	34,331	34,850	-18.9%	30
USA	20,110	22,890	19,440	20,100	20,550	2.2%	50
Argentina	15,460	15,220	15,400	15,050	14,680	-5.0%	65
China	11,108	11,536	11,963	12,390	13,005	17.1%	26
Australia	14,680	14,300	14,260	9,610	11,700	-20.3%	68
Germany	10,007	9,153	8,916	10,161	10,400	3.9%	102
South Africa	9,280	8,410	9,410	9,840	9,890	6.6%	75
Chile	6,300	7,890	8,450	8,280	7,860	24.8%	40
Romania	6,166	2,602	5,014	5,289	6,300	2.2%	31
Portugal	7,481	7,266	7,543	6,049	5,400	-27.8%	22
Greece	4,248	4,027	3,938	3,511	3,750	-11.7%	32
Brazil	3,930	3,200	2,370	3,500	3,500	-10.9%	35
Hungary	4,340	3,103	3,271	3,168	3,400	-21.7%	47
Austria	2,735	2,264	2,256	2,628	2,400	-12.2%	47
Bulgaria	1,949	1,708	1,757	1,796	1,800	-7.6%	19
New Zealand	1,190	1,020	1,330	1,480	1,700	42.9%	49

Sources: Elaborated from http://www.oiv.int/http://www.export.gov/tradedata/index.asp

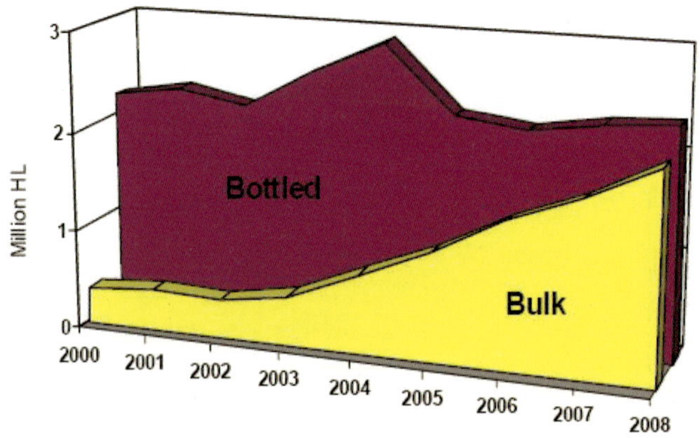

(Source : Office of Global Analysis, 2009)

Figure 14-1 USA Bulk Wine Exports Grew Faster Than Bottled

2) Major exporters

The leading wine exporters are shown in Table 14-2. Most wine is produced for domestic consumption. Of the leading wine producing countries, only Chile, Australia, and Portugal export more than 50% of production. However, for all of these countries, the export sector is large enough to be of great importance to their economies.

In relation to an increase in overall export quantities, recent years have seen a fall back in exports from Europe and progressive growth in exports from other production areas. However, Europe is the dominant exporter, accounting for about half of the world’s trade.

The world's number one wine exporter, Italy with about 20 million hl, exports more than 5 times as much wine as South Africa which is now the world's 8 largest exporter. France ranks second with more than 14, and Spain third with 14.

The fourth exporter is Australia, with more than 6 million hl, followed with less than 4 million hl respectively by Chile, USA, Argentina and South Africa. USA is the sixth largest exporter. Figure 14-1 shows that rising bulk exports, versus bottled, are less expensive to transport and give USA a competitive cost advantage (Office of Global Analysis, 2009).

Table 14-2 Wine exports of Leading Producers, 2008

Country	Volume (million hl)	% share in production
Italy	20.1	43.0%
France	14.1	32.8%
Spain	14.0	40.3%
Australia	6.4	55.1%
Chile	5.3	68.0%
USA	4.5	21.9%
Argentina	4.2	28.6%
South Africa	3.7	37.4%
Germany	3.6	35.1%
Portugal	2.8	51.2%
New Zealand	0.1	43.2%

Source: http://www.oiv.int/

3) Wine consumption

Consider first per capita consumption. The top 20 wine consuming nations per capita are presented in Table 14-3 below. While they include six of the largest wine producers, it is notable that New Zealand (20.53 per capita), Chile (17.31 per capita), USA (9.43 per capita), and South Africa (8.90 per capita) are not in the top 20 (See Table 14-2; Figure 14-2).

(Figure 14-2: Map of per capita wine consumption in the world in 2006
Source: http://strangemaps.wordpress.com/2009/04/27/377-planet-of-the-grapes/)

Table 14-3 Leading Per Capita Wine Consuming Nations, 2008

Country	Volume (liter)
Croatia	55.84
France	44.56
Georgia	44.09
Italy	42.56
Slovenia	38.30
Switzerland	36.91
Portugal	35.28
Austria	32.00
Argentina	30.10
Germany	29.37
Denmark	29.20
Hungary	27.70
Belgium-Luxembourg	26.60
Slovak Republic	25.33
Uruguay	24.64
Netherlands	23.64
Greece	23.57
Spain	23.53
Belarus	23.41
Australia	22.57
Korea, Republic of	1.30

Source: Elaborated from http://www.iwsr.co.uk/, National Tax Service(국세청)

Global wine consumption totaled 6.4 billion gallons last year, down 0.8% from 2007's level, after years of growth, attributing the drop to slowing world economies. It is obvious that the world economic crisis has played a role in lowering overall demand (Keller, 2009).

Table 14-4 Leading Countries, Total Wine Consumption, 2008

Country	Volume (million hl)
China	40.84
USA	37.21
France	36.17
Italy	33.26
Germany	32.30
United Kingdom	17.02
Argentina	15.55
Spain	13.62
Russian Federation	12.87
Japan	11.72
Korea, Republic of	0.03 (=32940 hl)

Source: http://www.iwsr.co.uk/

Table 14-4 presents information on the largest national markets for wine. The top four wine consuming nations, China, USA, France and Italy consume about half of the world's wine. It is notable that China, with average per capita consumption of only 2.35 bottles per year, consumes more wine than any other country. The decline in consumption in Europe offset growth in other countries, such as the China and USA, whose consumption passed France's and Italy's for the first time.

The global wine industry is in fundamental transition. While overall consumption is rising slowly, there are big shifts in consumption patterns. Over the course of the last 20 years wine sales of the so-called "New World"—Australia, Chile, USA, Argentina, South Africa, and New Zealand—have exploded in international markets.

The traditional wine drinking countries are consuming less, while non-traditional countries particularly in the English-speaking world and Asia are drinking more. It is in these non-traditional markets where new world producers—Australia, Chile, USA, Argentina, South Africa, and New Zealand—are winning the battle. The fact that new world producers are performing best in non-traditional markets is a considerable cause for optimism. The new world producers can be credited with bringing in millions of new consumers into the wine world in markets such as the UK, USA, Canada and Scandinavia (Foodandbeveragereports, n.d.).

Over the next two decades, it is likely that per capita and total wine consumption in Europe will fall as their populations age (Morss, 2009).

Note

- deteriorate : to become worse
- ease : to move or to make something move slowly and carefully in a particular direction or into a particular position
- marginally : slightly
- stand : to be at a particular point while subject to change or fluctuation
- hl (hectoliter) : a metric unit of volume or capacity equal to 100 liters
- to the fore : to public attention or into a noticeable position
- optimism : being hopeful and emphasizing the good part of a situation rather than the bad part; the belief that good things will happen in the future

4) Wine consumption in Korea

This article is based upon a report about market profile for wine in Korea prepared by New Zealand Trade and Enterprise Seoul supported by New Zealand Government. They are doing detailed market researches and finding resources for doing business in key markets around the world (New Zealand Trade and Enterprise Seoul, 2008). Let's look at it.

According to Datamonitor, the wine market in Korea was worth an estimated US$ 359.6 million in 2007, up from US$ 321.6 million in 2006. Still wines accounted for 80.5 percent of sales, sparkling wines a further 16.5 percent, and fortified wines the remaining 3 percent. Within the still wine category, red wine made up 81 percent of sales.

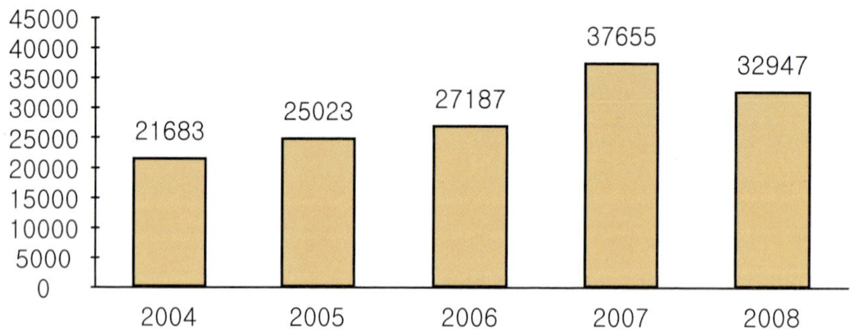

(Source : Elaborated from National Tax Service)

Figure 14-3 Wine Consumption in Korea (2004-2008) (Unit : kℓ)

Local companies produce wine, but the quantity and quality is low. A few companies import bulk wine from Spain, the US, Australia, Chile, Australia and Germany and bottle it locally. In 2005 Korea imported US$ 3.4 million worth of bulk wine and in 2006 it increased to US$ 3.9 million, and in 2007 it further increased by 33 percent to US$ 5.2 million.

In 2005 Korea imported US$ 64 million worth of bottled wine. In 2006 imports increased 32 percent to US$ 84 million, and in 2007 imports further increased by 70 percent to US$ 144 million. The current import market split by wine type is red wine (79.7%), white wine (14.8%) and sparkling wine (5.5%).

An increasingly westernized diet and drinking culture, rising incomes among middle and upper classes, and a perception that wine — in particular red wine — has health benefits have all contributed to the growth in wine consumption. The low alcohol percentage of wine compared to local and imported spirits, along with the enjoyable scent and taste of wine, is appealing to a younger generation Koreans, particularly women.

In the Korean market white wine was more popular than red wine until 1993. Media reports on the health benefits of red wine have shifted Korean customers' preferences from white to red wine.

Wine is permeating all levels of Korean society. According to NTS (National Tax Service) the concern on health and people regarding drinking wine as a sophisticated cultural activity boosted wine consumption (Yoon, 2008). Many people think that offering wine makes you look smart and sophisticated. A wide range of Koreans are interested in learning more about wine, so wine appreciation classes are always packed. Wine experts regularly write columns about wine in daily newspapers, weekly and monthly business magazines.

Wine has become one of the most popular gifts at Lunar New Year, Korean Thanksgiving and Christmas, because it is perceived as an upmarket, sophisticated, and elegant gift. Korea's leading economic think tank, Samsung Economic Research Institute, selected wine as one of the top 10 hit items in 2007 (See Figure 14-3).

There are currently more than 300 Korean companies importing wine into Korea and among them around 80 companies import regularly. These companies handle mainly European brands as Korean consumers like prestigious products and associate higher quality with well known European brands.

However, language barriers with European suppliers and difficulties understanding European labelling, together with increasingly competitively priced and higher quality wines from the US, Australia and Chile have resulted in importers increasing their purchases of non-European wines. Chilean wines in particular have increased market share in recent years since the FTA (free trade agreement) between Korea and Chile went into effect in April 2004 which allows Korean consumers a larger choice of good-value bottles. However France still dominates in all sectors as outlined below (See Table 14-5).

Table 14-5 % share of imported wine in 2007

Bottled sparkling wine (US$ 7,877,933)		Bottled red wine (US$ 114,462,900)		Bottled white wine (US$ 21,239,003)	
countries	& share	countries	& share	countries	& share
France	82%	France	41%	Italy	27%
Italy	8%	Chile	20%	France	25%
Spain	3%	US	12%	Germany	12%
		Italy	11%	Australia	9%
		Australia	7%	US	8%
				Chile	7%

(Source : Elaborated from New Zealand Trade and Enterprise)

Figure 14-3 shows that Korea has quickly emerged as a wine-drinking nation in recent years, but the bad economy is now apparently forcing credit-crunched wine lovers to rein in spending.

2009 was the first year since 1998 to mark an annual decrease in wine imports. However, there is a possibility that wine imports will rebound in 2010. With the free trade agreement (FTA) between Korea and the European Union expected to go into effect sometime during next year, bottles from European vineyards may become cheaper, as the 15 percent tariff on wines will be eliminated (Alibaba, 2009) (See Figure 14-4).

Imported bottles are tagged with a 15-percent duty and a further 30-percent liquor tax and a 10-percent education surtax, all before importers and retailers look for their margins. As a result, the prices of bottles often bloat by three-fold or more when they reach consumers.

Figure 14-4 Do you Know?

Note

- still wine : A term that applies to any wine that is not sparkling
- bulk wine : It refers to wine that's not yet packaged for retail sale.
- permeate : to spread through something and be present in every part of it
- sophisticated : knowledgeable about the ways of the world, self-confident, and not easily deceived
- appreciation : a full understanding of the meaning and importance of something
- upmarket : describes goods and products that are of very high quality and intended to be bought by people who are quite rich
- prestigious : very much respected and admired, usually because of being important
- go into effect : [for a law or a rule] to become effective
- emerge : to appear by coming out of something or out from behind something
- crunch a critical situation that arises because of a shortage (as a shortage of time or money or resources)
- rein sth in (also rein sth back) : to control an emotion, activity or situation to prevent it from becoming too powerful
- vineyard : a piece of land on which vines (= plants which produce grapes) are grown
- tariff : a charge or list of charges either for services or on goods entering a country

2. What does Sommelier do?

A sommelier is a wine expert who specializes in the restaurant side of the wine industry. A sommelier is trained in wine tasting, pairing wine with foods, wine purchasing, wine storage, and the creation of wine lists. Most of the finest restaurants employ at least one sommelier, and for the most prestigious resorts and restaurants, having a master sommelier is something of a necessity (Whatisabc, n.d.).

The core purpose of a sommelier is to ensure that dining patrons are able to find a wine within their budget that fits their tastes and complements their food. At the basic level, this means that a sommelier works with the kitchen to find suitable wines to pair with each entrée dish on the menu, and sometimes with other courses as well. At a higher level, a sommelier is often out on the floor of the restaurant, helping customers to decide the exact wine that best meets their needs (Hospitalityjobsireland, n.d.).

Note

- prestigious : very much respected and admired, usually because of being important
- be something of a sth : used to describe a person or thing in a way that is partly true but not completely or exactly

3. Wine Facts and Information

- A bottle of opened wine stored in the refrigerator lasts 6 to 16 times longer than it would if stored at room temp.
- Wine is mentioned 521 times in the Bible.
- Cork was developed as a bottle closure in the late 17th century. It was only after this that bottles were lain down for aging, and the bottle shapes slowly changed from short and bulbous to tall and slender.
- Wine has so many organic chemical compounds it is considered more complex than blood serum.
- It is the VERY slow interaction of oxygen and wine that produces the changes noticed in aging wine. It is believed that wine ages more slowly in larger bottles, since there is less oxygen per volume of wine in larger bottles. Rapid oxidation, as with a leaky cork, spoils wine.
- The lip of a red wine glass is sloped inward to capture the aromas of the wine and deliver them to your nose.
- "Still wine" does not come from a still. The phrase refers to wine without bubbles, which includes what is also referred to as table wine.
- The wine industry generates 145,000 jobs in California.
- The Manhattan cocktail (whiskey and sweet vermouth) was invented by Winston Churchill's mother.
- The Oldest Wine : The wreck of the TITANIC holds the oldest wine cellar in the world and despite the depth and wreckage, the bottles are still intact.

- Wine Toast : The word "toast," meaning a wish of good health, started in ancient Rome, where a piece of toasted bread was dropped into wine.
- The Age of Oak : 170 years is the average age of a French oak tree harvested for use in wine barrels.
- California is the fourth-largest wine producer in the world, after France, Italy, and Spain.
- One ton of grapes makes about 60 cases of wine, or 720 bottles. One bottle of wine contains about 2.8 pounds of grapes.
- Traditionally, wine was never stored standing up. Keeping the wine on its side kept the wine in contact with the cork, thereby preventing the cork from drying, shrinking, and letting in air. However, wine can be stored vertically if the bottle has an artificial cork.
- Enologists are wine chemists who analyze samples of wine and advise winemakers.
- Wine facilitated contacts between ancient cultures, providing the motive and means of trade. For example, the Greeks traded wine for precious metals, and the Romans traded wine for slaves.
- When a food and wine pair well together they have synergy. This can cause a third flavor that is different than the food and drink consumed separately.
- The cost of wine is not an indicator of quality as there are many factors that have an effect on the price of a wine.
- Eat the crackers. They help you clean your palate and absorb the alcohol.
- Four clusters of grapes produces one bottle of wine.

- Only 257 people on Earth have earned the title: Master of Wine.
- The largest-sized wine bottles are named after biblical kings.
- In the 1600's, French wine makers used oil-soaked rags as stoppers instead of corks.
- You can find the word vineyard(s) more than 100 times in the King James Bible.
- There are approximately 20 billion bottles of wine produced worldwide each year.

Note

- mention : to speak about something quickly, giving little detail or using few words
- bulbous : rounded and swollen-looking
- serum : the watery, colourless part of the blood, or this liquid taken from an animal and put into a human in order to fight an infection
- lip : a part of an edge of a container that is shaped to allow liquid to be poured easily from the container
- table wine : a wine which is not very expensive and is of average quality
- wreck : a vehicle or ship that has been destroyed or badly damaged
- intact : complete and in the original state
- vertical : standing or pointing straight up or at an angle of 90° to a horizontal surface or line
- facilitate : to make possible or easier
- cluster : a group of similar things that are close together, sometimes surrounding something
- biblical : in or relating to the Bible

4. Wine Tasting Guide

Have you ever wondered what exactly you are supposed to do when you taste wine? Well don"t worry, you don't need to analyze wine to enjoy it, but if you pay

attention to what you're tasting you'll find that you'll be better able to identify what you like or don't like in a wine. It's a lot like languages: You don't have to speak French to visit France, but if you know a few words, your enjoyment and experience can be greatly enhanced. These guidelines below will walk you through wine tasting step by step.

1) Preparation

Before you taste make sure there are no distracting odors in the room, like cooking smells or perfume. The only thing you should smell is the wine in your glass. Glasses should be clean and dry and filled with only a small sample of wine (about a quarter of the glass). Wines all have certain components and characteristics in common. When we taste, we use sight, smell and taste to recognize the above various components and to assess the quality and health of the wine. So let's give it a go.

2) Guidelines

① Appearance

A good look at the wine can tell us about the condition and even age of the wine.

- Clarity: is the wine clear and bright (as it should be) or is it hazy or murky?
- Intensity: is the colour pale or deep?
- Colour: hold the glass at an angle against a white background (table cloth or sheet of paper) and assess the colour in the middle of the bowl of the glass and at the rim. White wines start life pale and darken with age. Red wines starts out with a deep, bright purple and gradually turn ruby, mahogany and eventually brown as they age.

② Smell

Swirl the wine in your glass. This is done to mix oxygen in with the wine, which will soften the tannins of young wine. Swirling the wine in the glass allows its flavors and aromas to be liberated into the air, so give your glass a whirl and then take a deep sniff. Initially you should hold the glass a few inches from your nose. Then let your nose go into the glass. What are you looking for?

- Condition: does it smell clean and attractive or is there any mustiness or off-odor?

- Intensity: is the nose faint or pronounced?
- Character: what does it smell like? This may seem difficult initially, but you can do it. Just as you can tell the difference between the smell of bacon and coffee, you can also identify some of the possible smells in wine. Here are some things you may smell: fruit, grapes, lemon, grass, peaches, raspberries, blackcurrants, flowers, apples, vanilla, oak, smoke, plums and many, many more. Remember that there are no right or wrong answers, here. It's simply an exercise in thinking about what you're drinking.

③ Taste

Now the fun part—Take a sip of wine and swirl it around the mouth so that the wine is in contact with all parts of your mouth: tongue, gums, soft palate but do not swallow just yet. Even better, tilt the head forward so that the wine is behind the front teeth and then slurp air into the mouth over the wine. You can taste much more of the wine if you aerate it in this way. Continue tasting for a few seconds and then swallow the wine. How long does the "finish" last? (How long can you taste the wine after you swallow?) Do you like the tastes?

3) So what are you supposed to be looking for?

Sweetness: an easy one. Sweetness is immediately noticeable on the tip of the tongue. If there's no apparent sugar the wine is called "dry".

Acidity: very important if the wine is to be refreshing and balanced. Lemon juice and vinegar are acidic. Too much and the wine tastes too tart; too little and the wine is known as "flabby", tasting heavy and just not refreshing.

Alcohol: a vital component in wine, but one that shouldn't stand apart from the other elements if the wine is to be balanced. When the alcohol is too high, there will be a bit of a burning sensation after the wine is swallowed.

Tannin: a natural preservative found in grape skins and stalks, tannin is the stuff that makes young red wines seem harsh and leaves the mouth feeling dry. If you want to know how tannin feels when it's not in wine, brew some very strong black tea and you'll soon know! Tannin's role as preservative is extremely important in high quality red wines that are made to age for many years.

Body: an indicator of how the wine feels in the mouth. Pinot Noir or Beaujolais tend to feel quite light in the mouth while Bordeaux or Australian Shiraz tend to be full and dense. So, the progression for both reds and whites is light-bodied, to medium bodied, to full-bodied.

Fruit: the taste and intensity of the fruit in the mouth; generally, the better the wine, the more evident the fruit. Also, younger wines will often display more fruit than mature wine.

Length: how long the taste of the wine lingers in the mouth after swallowing is a good indication of the wine's quality: the longer the better.

4) Conclusions

Having considered the above elements, what did you think of the wine?

Quality: you might think it's obvious to say that a $100 bottle of wine is likely to be high quality and a $5 wine low quality, but the assessment of quality goes beyond this. A wine that looks clear and bright, has a pronounced, intense nose, shows good fruit and balanced acid, sweetness and alcohol, and has a long finish might be an inexpensive wine. It would be classified as good quality, though, because it is a good example of its type. So as your tasting progresses, question the wine. Is it a good example of its type?

Maturity: this is a measure of the wine's readiness to drink, which is not the same thing as its age. Many wines are made to be drunk as soon as they are bottled while others require years (or decades) of maturation in bottle to reach their optimum state. Simple wines, which are designed to be drunk young, will not improve with age. Rather they will deteriorate and be over the hill if kept too long.

Faults: Thankfully, modern winemaking practices have reduced most of the problems we used to commonly find in wine, but there's still one which affects around a small percent of bottles: bad corks. "Corked", the term used to describe the affliction, has nothing to do with cork floating in the wine, but rather (not to get too technical) a condition in which the wine has reacted with a substance in the cork, producing a musty, corky smell and taste, reminiscent of wet cardboard. The wine should always smell clean and appealing. The cork problem is the reason behind many wineries switching to synthetic closures or screw caps, which are now widely used with aromatic varietals like Sauvignon Blanc and Riesling. So don't be put off by a screw cap on your wine you see. It doesn't mean cheap wine, it means the winemaker is sick of cork problems and wants to preserve the freshness of the wine.

Note

- walk sb through sth : to slowly and carefully explain something to someone or show someone how to do something
- distracting : taking somebody's attention away from what he or she wants to do or ought to be doing
- give it a go : to try or attempt
- bright : Perfectly clear wine with no suspended particles. Bright colour is an important guide to the quality of the wine
- hazy : used to describe a wine that has small amounts of visible matter.
- murky : more than deeply colored; lacking brightness, turbid and sometimes a bit swampy. mainly a fault of red wines.
- deep : having layers of persistent flavor that gradually unfold with aeration
- rim : the outer, often curved or circular, edge of something
- start out : to begin your life, or the part of your life when you work, in a particular way
- ruby : a dark red precious stone
- mahogany : a dark red-brown wood used to make furniture
- swirl : to (cause to) move quickly with a twisting circular movement
- tannin : a drying, astringent sensation on the palate that is generally associated with heavier red wines
- liberate : to help someone or something to be free
- sniff : a quick breath in through the nose to smell something, or to stop liquid in the nose from coming out
- musty : Wines aged in dirty barrels or unkept cellars or exposed to a bad cork take on a damp, musty character that is a flaw
- faint : to feel weak, as if you are about to become unconscious
- pronounced : very noticeable or certain
- sip : to drink, taking only a very small amount at a time

- gums : either of the two areas of firm pink flesh inside the mouth which cover the bones into which the teeth are fixed
- not just yet : 아직은
- aerate : to add a gas to liquid, especially a drink
- finish : Aftertaste, or final impression the wine leaves; it can have a long finish or a short one (not desirable).
- dry : opposite of sweet; somewhat subjective in that tasters may perceive sweetness to varying degree.
- balance or balanced : A primary goal of every winemaker, this is the all-important ratio between the different components of a wine that make it pleasant. Acidity must balance with sweetness, oak and tannin should balance with fruit, and alcohol should balance with body and flavor. If all of the wine's desirable components are present in proper proportion, it becomes graceful, like the sounds of a symphony. Sometimes age will have an influence on a wine's balance.
- tart : sharp; acceptable if not too acidic.
- flabby : Soft, lacking acidity on the palate (when a wine loses acidity, it is referred to as 'flat').
- heavy : High in alcohol, very full-bodied
- preservative : a substance used to prevent decay in wood
- harsh : rough, biting character from excessive tannin or acid
- Beaujolais : A red wine made from the Gamay grape that is fermented for just a few weeks before being released on third Thursday of November.
- light : Refers to wines light in alcohol but also to texture and weight, how the wine feels in the mouth. Lightness is appropriate in some wines, a defect in others.
- full or full-bodied : This is a textural description for a wine that feels full and weighty in your mouth. Typically, wines of relatively high alcohol will have fuller bodies for balance.

- dense : generally a reference to color depth, but sometimes of depth of flavor.
- progression : when something or someone changes to the next stage of development
- question : to express doubts about the value of something or whether something is true
- deteriorate : to become worse
- over the hill : used for describing someone who is old and no longer useful or attractive
- corked (corky) : Smelling of cork rather than wine; due to a faulty cork.
- affliction : something that makes you suffer
- musty : smelling unpleasantly old and slightly wet
- reminiscent of sb/sth : making you remember a particular person, event or thing
- synthetic : describes products that are made from artificial substances, often copying a natural product
- closure : a device for closing an opening, e.g. a zipper or a cap on a bottle, or the place where the opening closes
- screw cap : A cap that screws onto the threaded mouth of a container such as a bottle or jar.
- Riesling : One of the most important white wine varietals in Germany and one of the most celebrated varietals worldwide. Wines made from Riesling are balanced with strong fruit flavors and sufficient acidity to make them long-lived. Riesling accounts for some of the world's finest sweet whites.
- don't be put off : 망설이지마라
- sick : causing or expressing unpleasant emotions

5. Wine and Food Paring

Wine is food.

What is food and wine pairing? It is the simple process of identifying wines with flavors and body that complement or contrast with the particular entrees you offer. Wine, made from grapes, is actually a food. Like other foods, wine has many distinct qualities; some wines are sweet, some fruity, and some, like a great steak, are heavy and robust.

They key principle that always applies is this: There is NO one right or "perfect" wine choice when pairing food and wine. The main goal should always be to enhance the dining experience. Here are 4 helpful hints when pairing wine & food.

① Identify the weights of the food and wine.

A food's body is similar to wine. Salads are light and crisp, while duck is typically richer and heavier. The following wines are ranked by their typical weight (heavy to light):

- Cabernet Sauvignon
- Zinfandel
- Syrah/Shiraz
- Merlot
- Pinot Noir
- Chardonnay
- Pinot Gris
- Sauvignon Blanc

② Match the weight of the food and wine.

Again, the wine should be as full-bodied as the food it is going to accompany. Keep in mind that food preparation can impact the food's weight. Take, for instance, breaded shrimp v. shrimp scampi. When shrimp is breaded, a portion of the shrimp's flavor is masked and shifts its weight down. When pairing wine, look for light-bodied wines that will not hide the flavors of the shrimp. In contrast, the shrimp scampi, sautéeed in butter and garlic, increases in weight and needs a heavier wine in order to be tasted through the strong scampi flavors.

③ Identify the dominant flavor of the food.

For example, a breast of chicken's dominant flavor is chicken. However, when a herb like rosemary is added by the chef, the rosemary usually becomes the dominant flavor. Many times, the dominant flavor will follow the "with" in a menu item. Examples are "pasta with a pesto sauce" or "rack of lamb with mint jelly."

④ Select wines with aromas and flavors that enhance the flavor of the food.

There are two common methods of selecting wines, those that complement the meal and those that contrast with the meal.

When choosing wines that "complement" the meal, the flavor in the food tends to match the same flavor in the wine, often highlighting other flavor complexities. For example, a Cabernet Sauvignon with hints of mint would complement a lamb with mint sauce.

Another way to choose good pairings is to "contrast" flavors. For example, let's serve the shrimp sauteed with olive oil and garlic. A good wine to pair is a crisp Chardonnay with lots of citrus. The citrus and acid in the Chardonnay contrast with the shrimp in much the same way as a twist of lemon would. It's like adding and extra ingredient to the dish. Contrasting wines with food uses a distinct flavor in the wine like an added seasoning.

6. Role of Wine in Preparing a Dish

What part does wine play in the preparation of a dish? Apart from its gastronomic qualities of flavor, wine puts all its nutritional virtues at the service of the cooking and digestion of food. Wine contains glycerine, so it helps to bind sauces, and less fat can be used. Wine is well flavored, and allows the cook to go easy on salt or omit it altogether. Wine contains tannin, particularly when it has been cooked, and stimulates digestion. Wine contains alcohol, but very little of it indeed once it has evaporated in being cooked. It stimulates the tastebuds, and thus the appetite. It brings out the flavor of food and helps the system to digest fat. And it is very good for morale (Toussaint-Samat, 1987).

Note

- body : The body of a wine generally refers to the weight or fullness of a wine in your mouth. Wines can be categorized as light in body, medium or full. It can refer to the differences in weight in your mouth, similar to that of water, a milkshake or oil. These differences come mostly from the alcohol content, glycerin, or, in the case of dessert wines, sugar.
- flavor : Describing how the wine tastes
- fruity : Aromas and flavors that come directly from the grape, rather than from the winemaking process or from the barrels in which the wine was aged.
- heavy : Heavy: Thick, too dark
- robust : Full bodied wine
- weight : A tasting term. When tasters refer to the weight of a wine, it means its body.

- light : Refers to wines light in alcohol but also to texture and weight, how the wine feels in the mouth. Lightness is appropriate in some wines, a defect in others.
- Cabernet Sauvignon : A powerful, tannic red grape of noble heritage; the base grape for many red Bordeaux
- Zinfandel : A popular grape in California of disputed origin; scientists say it is related to grapes in Croatia and southern Italy.
- Syrah/Shiraz : Australia's signature red-wine grape. Same as Syrah.
- Merlot : A lauded red grape popular in Bordeaux and throughout the world; large amounts of Merlot exist in Italy, the United States, South America and elsewhere.
- Pinot Noir : The prime red grape of Burgundy, Champagne and Oregon.
- Pinot Gris : Also called Pinot Grigio, this is a grayish-purple grape that yields a white wine with a refreshing character.
- Sauvignon Blanc : White grape that makes grassy dry wines all over the world. Also used in dessert wines. Same as Fume Blanc.
- full-bodied : Rich, mouth filling, weighty-textured wine
- accompany : to go with somebody
- light-bodied : A wine with delicate flavors, texture and aromas
- dominant : more important, strong or noticeable than anything else of the same type
- pesto sauce : a green auce which is used in Italian cooking, especially on pasta
- aromas : Smells in wine that originate from the grape
- rack : a large piece of meat cut from the neck of a sheep
- hint : a very small amount of something
- crisp : Fresh, brisk character, usually with high acidity
- Chardonnay : Arguably the best and most widely planted white wine grape in the world
- twist : the shape of or a piece of something which has been twisted

- apart from : except for something aside from something
- gastronomy : the practice or art of choosing, cooking, and eating good food
- virtue : (an) advantage or good thing
- at (someone's) service : ready to help or be of use
- bind : to cause to cohere or stick together in a mass, ex) Bind the dry ingredients with milk and eggs.
- go easy on something : to not take or use too much of something
- bring out :
- morale : the amount of confidence felt by a person or group of people, especially when in a dangerous or difficult situation

References

Toussaint-Samat, Maguelonne, 1987, "History of Food," translated by Anthea Bell, Barnes&Nobles, New York, 1992, p.277.

Anonymous, 2005, "THE WORLD OF WINE IN FIGURES (Excerpt from a press release at Vinitaly 2005)," Retrieved Jan. 19, 2010 from http://www.vinography.com/archives/downloads/1311-GBCS9%20Statistiche%20CT%20-%20excerpt.pdf

Alibaba, 2009, Wine Boom Turns to Gloom, Published: 08 Dec, Retrieved Jan. 6, 2010 from http://news.alibaba.com/article/detail/trade/100214009-1-wine-boom-turns-gloom.html

Foodandbeveragereports, "Modern consumption and market performance of new world wine," Retrieved Jan. 9, 2010 from http://www.foodandbeveragereports.com/products/jusd97578.html

Gallosonoma, "Wine & food paring guide," Retrieved Jan. 6, 2010 from http://www.gallosonoma.com/uploadedfiles/pairing_guide.pdf

Hospitalityjobsireland, Sommelier–Job Description, Retrieved Jan. 9, 2010 from http://hospitalityjobsireland.com/files/art_files/220.pdf

Keller, Greg, 2009, "World Wine Consumption Falls For First Time In Years," April 7, Retrieved Jan. 9, 2010 from http://www.huffingtonpost.com/2009/04/07/world-wine-consumption-fa_n_184112.html

Morss, Elliott, 2009, "The Global Economics of Wine: Past, Present, and Future," 4 August, Retrieved Jan. 9, 2010 from http://www.morssglobalfinance.com/the-global-economics-of-wine-past-present-and-future/

New Zealand Trade and Enterprise Seoul, 2008, "Market Profile for Wine in Korea," New Zealand Trade and Enterprise, Feb. Retrieved Jan. 6, 2010 from http://www.nzte.govt.nz/explore-export-markets/market-research-by-industry/Food-and-beverage/Documents/Wine-market-in-South-Korea.pdf

Office of Global Analysis, 2009, "WINE: WORLD MARKETS AND TRADE." USDA, Foreign Agricultural Service, April, Retrieved Jan. 19, 2010 from http://www.fas.usda.gov/htp/2009_4_2%20Wine%20Article.pdf

Towerhatch, "Wine Tasting Guide," Retrieved Jan. 4, 2010 from http://towerhatch.ie/towerhatch/images/pdf/wine_tasting_guide.pdf

Whatisabc, "What is a Sommelier?," Retrieved Jan. 6, 2010 from http://whatisabc.com/what-is-a-sommelier.htm

Yoon, Ja-young, 2008, "Koreans Turn to Mild Alcoholic Beverages," The Korea Times, 6 May

Retrieved Jan. 6, 2010 from http://encarta.msn.com/,

Retrieved Jan. 6, 2010 from http://www.merriam-webster.com/,

Retrieved Jan. 6, 2010 from http://dictionary.cambridge.org/,

Chapter **15**

Introduction to Coffee

Coffee-A Worldwide Culture

MAKE IT ! DRINK IT ! LOVE IT !

Exporting Countries	Importing Countries
Angola - Benin - Bolivia - Brazil- Burundi - Cameroon - Central African Republic -Colombia - Congo Democratic, Republic of - Congo, Republic of - Costa Rica - Côte d'Ivoire - Cuba - Dominican Republic - Ecuador - El Salvador -Ethiopia - Gabon - Ghana - Guatemala - Guinea - Haiti - Honduras - India - Indonesia - Jamaica - Kenya - Madagascar - Malawi - Mexico - Nicaragua - Nigeria - Panama - Papua New Guinea - Paraguay - Philippines - Rwanda - Tanzania - Thailand - Togo - Uganda - Venezuela, Bolivarian Republic of - Vietnam - Zambia - Zimbabwe	European Community (Austria, Belgium, Bulgaria, Cyprus, Czech Republic, Denmark, Estonia, Finland, France, Germany, Greece, Hungary, Ireland, Italy, Latvia, Lithuania, Luxembourg, Malta, Netherlands, Poland, Portugal, Romania, Slovakia, Slovenia, Spain, Sweden, United Kingdom) - Japan - Norway - Switzerland - United States of America

(Source : ICO Annual Review 2007/08)

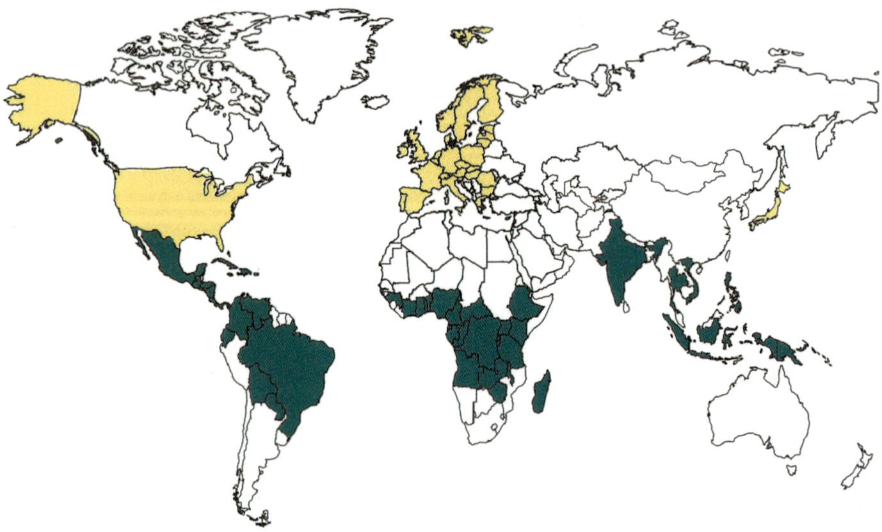

▌Figure 15-1▐ Coffee Exporting Countries & Importing Countries

1. Coffee Production and Consumption in the World

1) Coffee production

Table 15-1 shows that coffee is produced in more than 60 countries of which three account for more than half of the world's production: Brazil, Vietnam and Colombia. Arabica coffee, the fine-flavored, aromatic type makes up 60-65% of the total production and usually fetches the highest prices. The other variety, robusta, is easier to produce and is more resistant to disease (See Figure 15-1; 15-2).

Around 75% of all coffee is exported. Only Brazil and Indonesia enjoy high domestic consumption. The world's annual production is currently around 115 million 60-kg bags or 7 million tonnes. It takes 420,000 containers (20 ft.) to carry this much coffee. Placed in a row these would stretch over more than 2,500 km.

Table 15-1 Highest Coffee Production in 2008/2009
(Volume in 000 bags — % Share in World Production)

Brazil	45,992	35.9%
Vietnam	18,500	14.4%
Colombia	9,500	7.4%
Indonesia	8,638	6.7%
Mexico	4,650	3.6%
India	4,372	3.4%
Ethiopia	4,350	3.4%
Peru	3,868	3.0%
Guatemala	3,730	2.9%
Uganda	3,300	2.6%

(Source : Osorio, Néstor, 2009, "Outlook for the world coffee market 103rd Session," International Coffee Council, 21 to 25 Sep.)

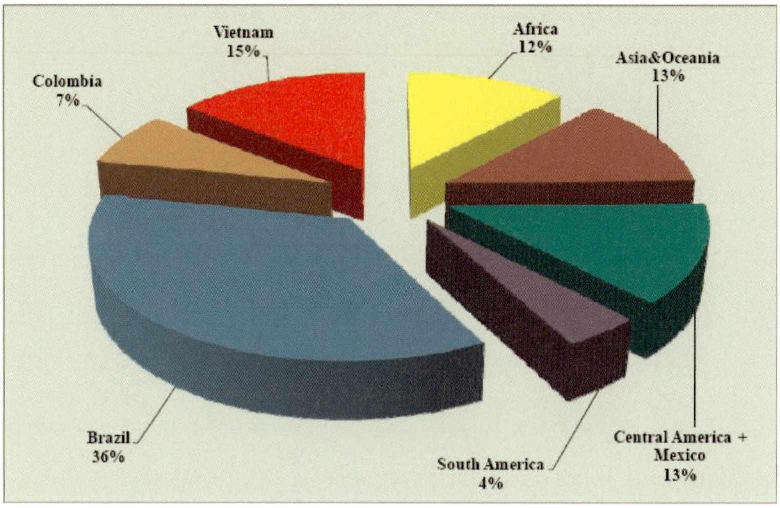

(Source : Osorio, Néstor, 2009, "Outlook for the world coffee market 103rd Session," International Coffee Council, 21 to 25 Sep.)

Figure 15-2 Total Production in 2008/09

2) Coffee consumption

Table 15-2 shows that the United States is currently the world's largest market for coffee. Annual consumption per capita is just over 4 kg compared with 5 kg on average in Europe. Consumption in Europe varies from around 10 kg per capita per year in the Nordic countries (Denmark, Finland, Iceland, Norway and Sweden) to around 3 kg in the United Kingdom and most of Eastern Europe.

Table 15-3 shows that the annual consumption of over 5 kg per capita in Brazil is exceptionally high among the over 60 coffee-producing countries. Brazil's annual production of around 2.4 million tonnes (40 million 60—kg bags) makes up a third of the world production of just over 7 million tonnes. (See Table 15-1; Figure 15-1; 15-2)

Table 15-2 Highest Coffee Consumption in 2008 (million bags)

Country	% Share in World Consumption
U.S.A.	21.7%
Brazil	17.9%
Germany	9.6%
Japan	7.1%
Italy	5.9%
France	5.1%
Russian Federation	3.7%
Spain	3.5%
Indonesia	3.3%
United Kingdom	3.1%
Korea, Republic of Korea	1.18% (2006 Data)

(Source : Osorio, Néstor, 2009, "Outlook for the world coffee market 103rd Session," International Coffee Council, 21 to 25 Sep.)

Table 15-3 List of Countries by Coffee Consumption Per Capita Per Year (2007)

Country	Amount (kgs)
Finland	12.0
Norway	9.9
Iceland	9.0 (2006 Data)
Denmark	8.7
Netherlands	8.4
Sweden	8.2
Switzerland	7.9
Belgium	6.8
Luxembourg	6.8
Aruba	6.8 (2006 Data)
Brazil	5.3
United States	4.2
Japan	3.3
Korea, Republic of	1.8 kgs

(Source : Elaborated from World Resource Institute. 2007 Data, http://earthtrends.wri.org/)

3) Coffee Consumption in Korea

Coffee consumption in Korea averages 1.3 million bags a year, accounting for 1.18% of the total consumption in the world (See Table 15-2). Korea's population is around 48 million and GDP per capita is estimated at US$20,100 in 2007. Table 15-4 shows that Korea has a fast growing economy and is one of the world's industrial emerging powers. Coffee consumption is, however, still not very widespread, since annual per capita consumption is around 1.8 kg and tea is still the main hot beverage consumed. Nonetheless, consumption has increased significantly over the last two decades (See Figure 15-3). Moreover, around 50% of the population is in the under-30s age group and this offers a promising prospect for

Table 15-4 Consumption in Top Emerging Markets from 1997-2007

	Volume (million bags)		Consumption Growth Rate
	1997	2007	
World Total	100.3	127.1	27%
Ukraine	0.17	1.06	533%
Sudan	0.10	0.49	390%
Russian Federation	1.86	4.05	118%
Turkey	0.24	0.52	118%
Syrian Arab Republic	0.21	0.44	108%
Serbia	0.31	0.61	100%
Algeria	1.46	1.97	35%
Korea, Republic of	1.06	1.42	34%
Australia	0.80	1.03	29%
Morocco	0.37	0.46	24%
Israel	0.37	0.44	20%

(Source : Osorio, Néstor, 2009, "Outlook for the world coffee market 103rd Session," International Coffee Council, 21 to 25 Sep.)

coffee consumption since young people tend to assimilate Western lifestyles, particularly in relation to eating habits, by moving away from the tea drinking tradition in favour of coffee. Since 2000, consumption has grown at an average annual rate of 2.4%. Imports originate mainly from Brazil, Colombia, Honduras, Indonesia and Vietnam (ICO, 2009).

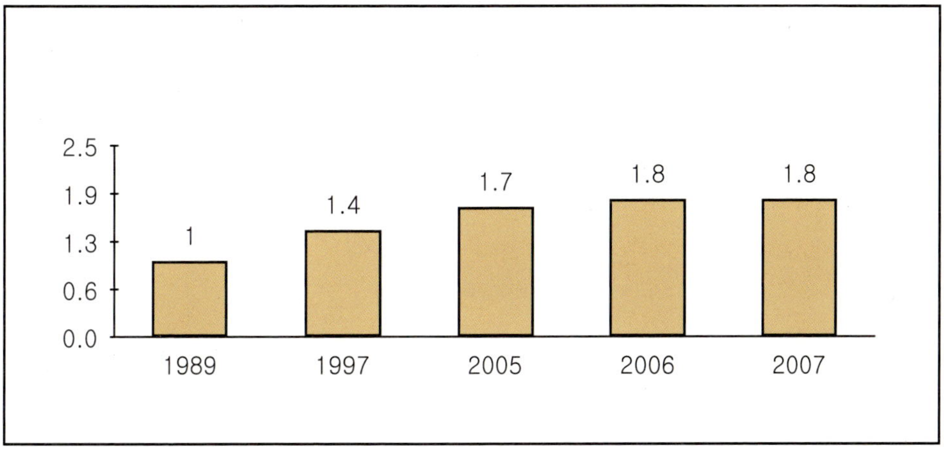

(Source : International Coffee Organization (ICO). 2008. Historical Coffee Statistics)

Figure 15-3 Coffee Consumption in Korea (1989 – 2007) (Unit : kg)

Note

- account for : to be responsible for something or be an important factor in something
- make up : to be a particular part or proportion of something
- fetch : to be sold for a particular amount of money
- per capita : If you state an amount per capita, you mean that amount for each person
- promising : Something which is promising shows signs that it is going to be successful or enjoyable
- assimilate : to take in, fit into, or become similar (to)

2. Knowledge about Coffee

1) Barista

If you were to visit a bar or coffeeshop in Italy, you might very well encounter a uniformed bartender called a barista. In Italy, a barista is a trained mixologist familiar with both alcohol and coffee-based drinks. He or she might even wear an elaborate jacket similar to that of a bandmaster or military officer. A barista is usually treated as a respected specialist, in the same vein as a wine steward or sommelier.

When the gourmet coffee industry exploded onto the scene during the 1980s and 1990s, however, the term barista took on a slightly different meaning. A barista in the coffeehouse sense is an expert in producing espresso and espresso-based drinks. Expresso is an intensely-flavored form of coffee generally served in a small cup called a demitasse. In order to brew a perfect cup of espresso, a barista must place a measured amount of ground coffee into a wire basket and tamp it down firmly. The wire basket is then locked under the spout of an espresso machine.

A trained barista should know precisely how much hot water should be forced through the mesh and for how long. If the time is too short, the espresso will be weak and watery. If the barista spends too much time, the espresso will be too strong to drink. It is this intimate knowledge of an espresso machine's capabilities that make a good barista indispensable to a coffeeshop. A barista may also have to create a good froth from steamed milk or allow the espresso to form a natural dark layer on top called a crema (Pollick, n.d.).

2) Arabica Coffee vs Robusta Coffee

There are two basic categories into which all species of coffee trees can be sorted. Although there are several varieties of each — each variety having its own character — this division into two large categories is useful for understanding the difference between a gourmet cup of coffee and an ordinary cup. High quality blends consist of 100% Arabica beans. Lower quality, cheaper blends may have some proportion of Robusta beans, or they may consist entirely of Robusta. Arabica beans produce a superior taste in the cup, being more flavorful and complex than their Robusta counterparts. Robusta beans tend to produce a more bitter brew, with a musty flavor and less body. This distinction being made, you can see why high quality coffees should consist of 100% Arabica beans.

Table 15-5 Types Of Coffee: Arabica, Robusta

Type	Arabica	Robusta
Growing Area	▸ Central America (Mexico, Guatemala, El Salvador, Nicaragua, Costa Rica, Panama) ▸ South America (Venezuela, Colombia, Ecuador, Peru, Bolivia, Paraguay, Argentina) ▸ India ▸ Eastern Africa (Ethiopia, Kenya, Tanzania, Zambia, Mozambique) ▸ Papua New Guinea	▸ Western and Central Africa (Ivory Coast, Cameroon, Uganda, Angola, etc.) ▸ Malaysia (Vietnam, Sri Lanka, Sumatra, Java, etc.) ▸ Brazil ▸ India
Growing Altitude	at higher altitudes, 1000 to 2000 meters	at lower altitudes, 0 to 700 meters
Caffeine Content	0.8 to 1.4%	1.7 to 4.0%
% share in world production	70%	30%

(Elaborated from : http://www.anothercoffee.co.uk/coffeeinfo/coffeetypes.aspx)

So why use Robusta at all? Well, there are several reasons these beans are grown and used. First of all, we have the economical concerns driving the farmer to grow the crop. Robusta coffee trees produce their first crops within about two to three years of being planted. Arabica trees require about four to five years to produce any fruit. So the farmer has an inducement to grow the faster growing variety to take advantage of upswings in the price of coffee. Also, the Robusta coffee tree can grow under a larger variety of environmental conditions than can the Arabica. It is more tolerant of cold and grows well in a wider range of altitudes. Second, roasters buy the beans because they are generally cheaper than the Arabica beans. They can be sold to less discriminating consumers in the pre-roasted, pre-ground, pre-staled cans of supermarket "coffee." They can be brewed and freeze-dried to make instant "coffee" without worrying about degrading an already questionable flavor. They can be used in blends with Arabica beans to make the blend cheaper for the roaster while still being able to make the claim that the blend includes Arabica beans. Finally, Robusta beans are higher in caffeine than Arabica beans and fuel the addiction many of us already suffer from (Kaffee, n.d.). (See Table 15-5)

3) Commercial vs Gourmet coffee

Gourmet coffee is made from Arabica Beans. These are the most flavorful beans. Commercial coffees are made from a mixture of Arabica and Robusta. Robusta beans are cheaper than Arabica beans, so the large commercial coffee manufacturers tend to use these beans in their blends and add a few Arabica beans for flavor. When the coffee prices go up, the commercial manufactures tend to use less of the Arabica bean in their mixture. Another disadvantage with commercial coffee is the freshness. The coffee sits on the shelf for more than two weeks and it may take a week or more to get to the stores shelves after it has been packaged. The major advantage of the commercial coffee is the price. It is definitely less expensive than the Gourmet coffees.

Gourmet coffee is roasted and sold within a one week period. It is usually sold in the whole bean form. This way it retains its flavor until you decide to brew it. Unlike commercial coffees, you can choose origin (Sumatra, Kona, etc..) and the type of roast (French, Italian, Light, etc..). Gourmet coffees offer the consumer more choices than the commercial manufacturers. The major advantage of gourmet coffees is flavor (Coffeechronicle, n.d.).

4) Specialty Coffee

There are two major species of coffee, robusta and arabica. All of the world's great coffees are 100% arabica, but only the top 10% have fine enough flavor to be selected as specialty coffee. The fine flavor is determined by the cupping score. To be considered specialty, the cupping score must be at least 80, using the SCAA criteria (Invalsa, n.d.).

Note

- mixologist : the art or skill of preparing mixed drinks
- vein : a style or a temporary mood
- scene : the characteristic environment in which an activity or pursuit is carried out
- measured : determined as a result of measuring
- tamp down : press down tightly
- spout : a tube-shaped opening which allows liquids to be poured out of a container
- mesh : (a piece of) material like a net with spaces in it, made from wire, plastic or thread
- intimate : expert, detailed and obtained from a lot of studying or experience
- indispensable : Something or someone that is indispensable is so good or important that you could not manage without them
- gourmet : of food) very high quality
- brew : a mixture of several things
- musty : smelling unpleasantly old and slightly wet
- body : a strong or thick quality
- inducement : an act or thing that is intended to persuade someone or something
- upswing : an increase or improvement
- tolerant : willing to accept behaviour and beliefs which are different from your own, although you might not agree with or approve of them
- altitude : height above sea level
- discriminating : able to know and act on the difference between good and bad
- pre-staled (degassed) : to remove gas from
- fuel : to stimulate or maintain something, especially an emotion
- cupping : It is a professional technique for evaluating coffee's Fragrance/Aroma, Flavor, Acidity, Body and Aftertaste. To be considered specialty or premium, coffee must exhibit distinct attributes in these five areas. Moreover, such coffee must be free from odors, faults and taints.
- SCAA : the Speciality Coffee Association of America

Table 15-6 Global Coffee Traditions

Area	Traditions
Northern Europe	All kinds of coffee and milk-based coffees in big cups
Southern Europe	Small cups of strong espresso
Africa	Coffee from high-quality beans
North America	Take-away coffee and flavored coffees
South America	Traditional filtered coffee, especially in Brazil
Asia	Canned coffee (hot and cold) out of streetside vending machines in Japan, milky sweet coffee from a syrupy "decoction" in India and an entrenched preference for tea in China
Middle East	Traditional Arabic coffee served the regional way—boiled and in small cups

(Source : Elaborated from Simmons, 2009)

3. Coffee Trivia

- Coffee was first known in Europe as Arabian Wine.
- The heavy tea tax imposed on the colonies in 1773, which caused the "Boston Tea Party," resulted in America switching from tea to coffee. Drinking coffee was an expression of freedom.
- Coffee statistics show that coffee is the most popular beverage worldwide with over 400 billion cups consumed each year.
- Coffee industry statistics show that only 20% of harvested coffee beans are considered to be a premium bean of the highest quality.

- Coffee market statistics show that coffee is grown commercially in over 45 countries around the world.
- Coffee trade statistics show that over 5 million people in Brazil are employed by the coffee trade; most of those are involved with the cultivation and harvesting of more than 3 billion coffee plants.
- Coffee consumption statistics show that coffee represents 75% of all the caffeine consumed in the United States.
- Bach wrote a coffee cantata in 1732. Cantata is a Italian word meaning "To sing."
- In the year 1763, there were over 200 coffee shops in Venice
- Italy now has over 200,000 coffee bars, and still growing.
- The first commercial espresso machine was manufactured in Italy in 1906.
- Espresso is to Italy what champagne is to France.
- In Italy, coffee and espresso are synonymous.
- Coffee shops make up the fastest growing part of the restaurant business, checking in with a 7% annual growth rate!
- World coffee production is estimated at 110—120 million bags per year!
- 14 billion espresso coffees are consumed each year in Italy, reaching over 200,000 coffee bars, and still growing!
- Americans consume 400 million cups of coffee per day, or equivalent to 146,000,000,000 (146 Billion) cups of coffee per year; making the United States the leading consumer of coffee in the world.

- Japan ranks number 4 in the world for coffee consumption.
- Café Bars average sales of 230 cups a day.
- Germany is the world's second largest consumer of coffee in terms of volume at 16 pounds per person.
- Over 53 countries grow coffee worldwide, but all of them lie along the equator between the tropic of Cancer and Capricorn.
- An acre of coffee trees can produce up to 10,000 pounds of coffee cherries. That amounts to approximately 2,000 pounds of beans after hulling or milling.
- The percolator was invented in 1827 by a French man. It would boil the coffee producing a bitter tasting brew. Today most people use the drip or filtered method to brew their coffee.
- With the exception of Hawaii and Puerto Rico, no coffee is grown in the United States or its territories.
- Up until the 1870's most coffee was roasted at home in a frying pan over a charcoal fire. It wasn't until recent times that batch roasting became popular.
- Each year some 7 million tons of green beans are produced world wide. Most of which is hand picked.
- 27% of U.S. coffee drinkers and 43% of German drinkers add a sweetener to their coffee.
- Hard bean means the coffee was grown at an altitude above 5000 feet.
- Arabica and Robusta trees can produce crops for 20 to 30 years under proper conditions and care.

- Most coffee is transported by ships. Currently there are approximately 2,200 ships involved in transporting the beans each year.
- The popular trend towards flavored coffees originated in the United States during the 1970's.
- October 1st is the official Coffee Day in Japan.
- The first coffee tree in the Western Hemisphere was brought from France to the Island of Martinique in the 1720's.
- Coffee accounts for over 93% of all the caffeine consumed in the world today.
- Coffee commands an average price of $2.00 a cup. The Coffee grower gets 1 cent.
- Coffee is the second most valuable traded commodity on earth followed only by oil.
- The average age of an Italian barista is 48 years old. A barista is a respected job title in Italy.
- In the last three centuries, 90% of all people living in the Western world have switched from tea to coffee.
- The world can be divided into nations of coffee drinkers and nations of tea drinkers.
- The Europeans first added chocolate to their coffee in the 1600's.
- Frederick the great had his coffee made with champagne and a bit of mustard.
- Finely grinding coffee beans and boiling them in water is still known as "Turkish Coffee." It is still made this way today in Turkey and Greece or

anywhere else Turkish Coffee is served.

- The French philosopher, Voltaire, reportedly drank fifty cups of coffee a day.
- After they are roasted, and when the beans begin to cool, they release about 700 chemical substances that make up the vaporizing aromas.
- Italians do not drink espresso during meals. It is considered to be a separate event and is given its own time. (See Table 15-6)
- In Italy, espresso is considered so essential to daily life that the price is regulated by the government. (See Table 15-6)
- Iced coffee in a can has been popular in Japan since 1945. (See Table 15-6)

Note

- trivia : details or information that are not important
- harvest : to pick and collect crops, or to collect plants, animals or fish to eat
- premium : describes something that is of higher than usual quality
- synonymous : having the same meaning
- check in : announce one's arrival, e.g. at hotels or airports
- equator : an imaginary line drawn around the middle of the Earth an equal distance from the North Pole and the South Pole
- the Tropic of Cancer : the northern tropic
- the Tropic of Capricorn : Capricorn
- hull : to remove the covering or the stem and leaves from some fruits, vegetables and seeds
- mill : to crush grain into flour or another substance into powder
- percolator : a device for making coffee in which hot water passes through crushed coffee beans into a container below
- drip : to produce drops of liquid

- batch : a group of things or people dealt with at the same time or considered similar in type
- Martinique : an island in the eastern Caribbean in the Windward Islands
- command : to deserve or be entitled to something
- commodity : a substance or product that can be traded, bought or sold
- vaporize : to turn, or cause something to turn, from a solid or liquid state into gas

4. An interesting Story of Coffee

Today's show is brought to you by COFFEE. Actually everyday's show is brought to you by coffee, because without it I would not be able to get out of the house in the morning! The story of coffee is actually a really interesting history of international trade and relations between countries (Outreachworld, unknown era).

The Arabic word for coffee is qahwah, this word went into Turkish as kahve (Turkish does not have a W sound,) and from that we get the words cafe and coffee. Qahwah is actually an old Arabic word which was another name for wine, but eventually after coffee was introduced it came to mean just coffee. From this we also get words like caffeine and cafeteria.

The coffee plant is a small tree which actually originated in the mountains of Ethiopia. The beans were used as both a food and to make the drink. From Ethiopia, the Yemenis brought it over and planted it in Yemen, almost 600 years ago. The Ethiopians called the tree, the coffee beans, and the drink made from them "Bunn," and that became the name of the beans in Arabic. I think it's just a coincidence that "bunn" sounds like "bean."

From Yemen, coffee began to be exported all over the Arab world, and later to Turkey and Iran. The main port from which coffee was exported was the city of al-Mukhaa. And that's where we get the word Mocha as a name for coffee. So coffee growing started in Ethiopia, went over to Yemen, and for about 200 years Yemen was the most important coffee-growing center. Then in the 1600's coffee started to become popular in Europe, and European merchants started to get in on the coffee trade. The Yemenis grew very rich from the demand for coffee in Europe, and prices were high. So the Europeans figured they could break the Yemeni monopoly on coffee by growing the tree in other places. They had lots of colonies, so the Dutch smuggled plants to Indonesia and started growing it there, and the British took the plants to Nigeria and Jamaica. Even so, Yemen remained the center of the world coffee trade for hundreds of years.

There's a lot of talk today about "globalization." The story of coffee is an amazing example of this. From its origins in Ethiopia, coffee is now grown in about 50 countries around the world, and some 25 million people around the world depend on coffee to make their living. Do you know what country produces the most coffee today? It's not Yemen. It's actually Brazil. When you go to buy coffee, you usually find it called by the country it's grown in, such as Ethiopia, Colombia, Sumatra, Java, Guatemala, Nicaragua, Nigeria, Kenya, Jamaica, El Salvador, Costa Rica, and Mexico. These are some of the best-known varieties of coffee.

An interesting subject in the history of coffee is its relationship with the religion of Islam. You probably know that Islam prohibits drinking alcohol, or taking any other intoxicating substances. So when coffee first started becoming popular, there was a big debate about whether it was legal or not, because of course it has an effect on the body. This went back and forth over more than a hundred years, and sometimes coffee was made illegal, and then the next ruler would decide that it was legal after all. Eventually coffee became accepted as Islamically permitted by almost everybody. One of the earliest uses of coffee was actually as a medicine, although there was also a debate as to whether it was helpful or harmful. And you know, that debate is still going on today.

Coffeehouses are very popular in the Arab world. People (mostly men) go and sit and hang out with their friends and drink tea or coffee, play backgammon or dominoes. Arabs today actually drink more tea than coffee. In the past, storytellers would come and tell stories in the coffeehouses, but now most of the story tellers are gone and people just listen to the radio or watch TV.

The traditional Arab method of making coffee is to grind the roasted beans really fine, and boil them for a while in the coffeepot, called a dallah. In much of the

Arab world, the easier way is to take a spoonful of the ground bunn and mix it with water in a kanakah, and bring it to a boil over the stove. It's drunk in small cups, called "finjaan." Some people like it with sugar and some without, but you never add milk. Either way you produce what the Arabs call Arabic coffee, and what people in the West usually call Turkish coffee. Often it is mixed with the spice called cardamom. (hayl or abb al-haan in Arabic) Cardamom comes in little seed pods. It is ground up and brewed with the coffee. Cardamom was and still is an expensive spice, more expensive than coffee itself, so using cardamom was considered a luxury. The wealthier you were, the more cardamom you used in your coffee, until if you were really wealthy, or as a sign of your hospitality, you served your guests coffee that was only about 10% coffee and 90% cardamom—in fact it doesn't look like coffee at all—it's much yellower and more perfumy. You can get cardamom at most grocery stores. If you grind your own beans for coffee, you can add a few cardamom pods to give your coffee the "Arabic flavor." If you use a coffee filter, you can just grind up the whole pod with your beans. If you want to mix the cardamom directly with the beans in the water, in a kanakah, you will need to take the little seeds out of the pod husk first.

Note

- Turkish : relating to the language of Turkey
- originate : to come from a particular place, time, situation, etc
- coincidence : an occasion when two or more similar things happen at the same time, especially in a way that is unlikely and surprising
- get in : to become involved with a group or in an activity, or let somebody become involved
- Yemeni : a native or inhabitant of Yemen
- figure : to expect or think that something will happen

- monopoly : (an organization or group which has) complete control of something, especially an area of business, so that others have no share
- colony : a country or area controlled politically by a more powerful and often distant country
- Dutch : the people of the Netherlands
- smuggle : to take things or people to or from a place secretly and often illegally
- living : the money that you earn from your job
- Islam : the Muslim religion, and the people and countries who believe in it
- prohibit : to prevent somebody from doing something
- intoxicating : capable of making somebody drunk or stupefied
- back and forth : the repeated exchange of ideas, opinions, or information
- Islamically : 이슬람교도 원리로
- hang out with somebody : to spend time with someone
- backgammon : a game for two people in which you throw dice and move circular pieces around a special board with narrow triangular shaped patterns on it
- dominoes : a game using dominoes
- Arab : a person from the Middle East or North Africa who speaks Arabic as a first language
- kanakah : a brass pot
- cardamom : the aromatic pods and seeds of a tropical plant, used whole or crushed as a spice or flavoring
- come in : to arrive or be received and become available for use, sale, or communication
- pod : a long, narrow, flat part of some plants, such as beans and peas, which contains the seeds and usually has a thick skin
- hospitality : kindness in welcoming guests or strangers
- perfumy : used for the perfume-like aroma that is emitted from certain cheeses. Aged Goudas and Gruyères often have this characteristic.
- husk : the dry outer covering of some seeds

References

Coffeechronicle, "COMMERCIAL vs. GOURMET COFFEE," Retrieved Jan. 20, 2010 from http://www.coffeechronicle.com/commer.htm.

ICO, 2009, "Study on coffee consumption in ICO non-member countries," International Coffee Council 102nd Session 18, 20 March, London, England, Retrieved Jan. 20, 2010 from http://www.unctad.org/sections/wcmu/docs/ditc_comb_Coffee003_en.pdf

Invalsa, "What is "Specialty" Coffee," Retrieved Jan. 6, 2010 from http://www.invalsa.com/specialty_coffee.php

Kaffee, "Robusta vs. Arabica," Retrieved Jan. 6, 2010 from http://kaffee.netfirms.com/Coffee/robustavsarabica.html

Osorio, Néstor, 2009, "Outlook for the world coffee market 103rd Session," International Coffee Council, 21 to 25 Sep, Retrieved Jan. 5, 2010 from http://dev.ico.org/presents/0809/market09.pdf

Outreachworld, "LESSON 50 COFFEE!!!! COFFEE COFFEE COFFEE!!!," Retrieved Jan. 4, 2010 from http://www.outreachworld.org/Files/Curriculum/Coffee.pdf

Pollick, Michael, "What is a Barista?," Retrieved Jan. 6, 2010 from http://www.kickbuttcoffee.com/what-is-a-barista.htm

Retrieved Jan. 7, 2010 from http://encarta.msn.com/encnet/features/dictionary/

Retrieved Jan. 4, 2010 from http://www.top100espresso.com/coffee_consumption_statistics_report.html

Retrieved Jan. 4, 2010 from http://www.coffee-statistics.com/coffee_statistics_ebook.html

Retrieved Jan. 4, 2010 from http://www.merriam-webster.com/,

Retrieved Jan. 4, 2010 from http://dictionary.cambridge.org/,

Retrieved Jan. 4, 2010 from http://www.anothercoffee.co.uk/coffeeinfo/coffeetypes.aspx)

저자 : 강경재(姜炅宰)

- 전북대학교 졸업(학사)
- 호원대학교 졸업(학사)
- 경기대학교 대학원 관광경영학과 졸업(경영학 석사)
- 경기대학교 대학원 관광경영학과 졸업(경영학 박사)
- 전 군산 미공군기지 제8헌병대대 언어전문관
- 전 경기대학교, 호원대학교, 남서울대학교, 혜전대학, 혜천대학, 군장공업대학, 원광보건대학 강사
- 전 혜전대학 호텔조리계열 학부장
- 전 혜전대학 호텔조리외식계열 계열장
- 전 혜전대학 호텔조리외식계열 음료경영전공 전공장
- 현 혜전대학 호텔조리외식계열 일식전공 전공장

[저서 및 논문]
- 신관광영어강독, 학문사(1998)
- Hotel & Food Service Cuisine English, 백산출판사(1999)
- Guide to the Student Chef, 대왕사(2001)
- Guide to Culinary English, 대왕사(2003)
- Guide to Food Styling English, 대왕사(2005)
- Guide to Recipe for the Student Chef, 대왕사(2006)
- Guide to Culinary and Foodservice English, LBH(2007)
- Guide to Kitchen English, 백산출판사(2008)
- Guide to Recipes of Oriental Cuisines, 대왕사(2009)
- 「호텔 레스토랑의 데이터베이스 마케팅에 관한 연구」 외 다수

Guide to the Culinary Industry

2010년 2월 24일 초판 인쇄
2010년 2월 27일 초판 발행

저 자 강 경 재
발행인 (寅製) 진 욱 상
발행처 백산출판사
서울시 성북구 정릉3동 653-40
등록 : 1974. 1. 9. 제 1-72호
전화 : 914-1621, 917-6240
FAX : 912-4438
http://www.ibaeksan.kr
edit@ibaeksan.kr
biz@ibaeksan.kr

저자와 합의하에 인지첩부 생략

이 책의 무단복사 및 전재는 저작권법에 저촉됩니다.

값 20,000원
ISBN 978-89-6183-299-1